SUSTAINABILITY:

Personal To Global

―――

Toward A Healthier Enriched Lifestyle

Heath J. Carney

Table of Contents

Foreword

The idea for this book began as I prepared college courses, training classes and public presentations over the years. I have taught undergraduate biology, human health, and environmental science courses since the 1980s. Sustainability made all these subjects more timely and relevant, so I included this topic in these courses. I have also given presentations, trainings and workshops to working adults on sustainability topics covered in this book. That is when I realized how significant this subject is for all of us, not just college students, throughout our lives. I have also found that this is a powerful approach for improving our lifestyles.

Recently my mother asked me to recommend a sustainability book which she could give to my niece as a Christmas present. I could list many specialized professional books which would be of limited interest. I could also suggest some "classics" which are great historical references but not necessarily timely. That is why this book is urgently needed! The goal of this book is to make sustainability clear and accessible to a broad range of readers, from young adult to senior. I do this with a strong conceptual foundation and many positive practices which the reader can incorporate into a more fulfilling and sustainable lifestyle.

My sustainability adventures began in the 1970s. They then grew to more professional efforts during the 1980s. This included work with United Nations (UNESCO, UNDP and UNEP) projects and programs outlined in Brundtland (1987) and Rio Earth Summit (1992). I found that sustainability was providing a very productive framework for these efforts. I was able to implement research projects that were compatible with both conservation and development goals in regions of California and Latin America.

At that time, penetration to the private sector and ultimately the individual consumer was quite limited. During the late 1990s I began to gain experience in the private sector. I helped introduce greener vehicles into the California market. This include the hybrid Toyota Prius in the early 2000s, and then the plug-in electric Chevrolet Volt in late 2010. This impressed upon me how important it is for consumers to understand and appreciate new green technologies, and then support great products. I have been in contact with thousands of customers, and participated in presentations and events for thousands more. Many questions and conversations were about best links to the home, clean energy sources and more sustainable lifestyles. This book presents my answers and positive solutions inspired by all these discussions. Four key chapters quite relevant for all our lives are Food, Water, Home and Mobility. They recapitulate my many projects and life experiences which began with food, continued with water and sustainable communities, and lead to electric vehicles and related new clean technologies.

There are many books on specialized and advanced topics of sustainable development and business. These books are very interesting and informative at the global and regional scales. Still, they are not immediately relevant or accessible to most of us at the level of our everyday lives. That is why I focus in the following chapters on what can be done at the individual level. This complements efforts at regional and global levels so the full potential of sustainability can be realized. As we see how sustainability concepts and practices can improve our lives, they can fuel more progress at larger scales. Thus my goal here is to demonstrate both material and psychological benefits at the individual level. These practices and their benefits change over time with improving technologies and new conditions. Thus I present a general guide and approach rather than hard and fast rules and technologies. Readers can then make adjustments to their individual circumstances. My main goal is to make this subject practical and fulfilling, so enjoy and prosper!

Acknowledgements

My parents Stephen and June Carney provided me a remarkable childhood which included many moves to countries in three continents (Europe, North America and South America). This was challenging at times, yet ultimately quite rewarding with lifelong impacts that contributed to my appreciation and understanding of sustainability. I grew up in a great diversity of regions: coastal to mountain, temperate to tropical, and developing to developed. I experienced first-hand the very significant challenges some of these regions are facing. I also appreciated the ingenious cultural adaptations and solutions of people to their regions. These experiences have certainly influenced the perspective on sustainability I express in this book.

During the seventies, I had the opportunity to work with Stephen Brush, Anthropologist and Human Ecologist, as an undergraduate research assistant on agricultural biodiversity in the Andes. This combined social with environmental and biological sciences, so I consider this a sustainability project long before the term was popularized.

I then came to California for graduate work with Peter Richerson and Charles Goldman of University of California-Davis on projects in Latin America and California. This eventually lead to collaboration with Michael Binford and Richard Forman, Graduate School of Design, Harvard, and many others including Alan Kolata on an Andean raised field agricultural sustainability project.

Shortly after arriving in California, Sandra Carroll introduced me to Village Homes. Over the years I got to know the developer Michael Corbett and many neighbors who were dedicated to this wonderful community. I found this to be an ideal location to learn and practice a sustainable lifestyle, and so lived there nearly two decades.

Since 1999, Dave Rodgers and John Sullivan supported my interest and contributions to greener vehicles. This began with conventional hybrids and then continued with plug-in electric models. This included sales, promotions, events, and training/education. The following have helped me maintain focus on the consumer: Tim Hastrup and Guy Hall of SacEV, Chelsea Sexton and Eric Cahill of Plug In America, and Chuck Golden, head of the Green Dealer Support program.

The following have supported this book and provided very helpful comments on certain chapters: Fee Yee, Fion Chu, Kevin Favro, Brian Carney, Trisha Badger and Kevin Carney, Lee Collins, Madeleine Collins, Ric Carney, Jing Zhang, and Stephen Brush. Michelle Hamilton, June Carney, Madeleine Collins, James and Sandee Cochran have improved clarity and relevance for a broad audience. Nida Javaid provided excellent and timely technical help with figures, tables, and final formatting of the manuscript.

Finally I especially thank my partner Fee who has been my Muse during the final preparation of this book. Her unwavering loving support and grace helped me through the many ups and downs of the manuscript. She has inspired my effort to add a personal and loving approach to sustainability which I hope comes through clearly to you.

Dedicated To

M y parents, family and friends who have shared my sustainability adventures,

Those striving to apply sustainability to their lifestyles and work,

Especially: younger and future generations that can and will benefit most from our sustainability efforts.

Four Generations Of The Carney Family

Chapter One

INTRODUCTION AND HISTORICAL BACKGROUND

———

This book addresses the most significant issues of our time with practical solutions you can make part of your daily life. The main goal is to improve your life, and in the process contribute to the solutions of larger regional and global issues. To date, most sustainability and sustainable development thinking and efforts have been at the global and regional levels to address enormous global issues including climate change, loss of biodiversity, air and water quality, depletion of soils and other resources, and population growth (see Table 1.1 for a summary). All these issues have been analysed and discussed in detail. One of the most notable global summaries is <u>The Age Of Sustainable Development</u> by Jeffrey Sachs (2015). Organizations such as United Nations and Worldwatch Institute provide annual

Table 1.1. Summary of major global trends.

Human population growth	The global human population has reached 7.8 billion in 2020, with projected increases of about 70 million per year.
Climate change, greenhouse gas emissions and air quality	While weather can be quite variable, long-term increases in greenhouse gases, air and water temperatures are clear. Carbon dioxide concentrations in the air have climbed steadily from about 310 ppm in 1960 to currently over 400 ppm. Historically, unhealthy air pollution has been especially evident in larger cities such as Los Angeles and Beijing. Globally, it kills 6.5 million people per year.
Land transformation and loss of biodiversity	Forests still cover about 30% of total land area. There is special concern about deforestation in tropical and subtropical regions where it is currently greatest. These forests have especially beneficial ecosystem services including carbon capture. They also harbor very high biodiversity. Globally, species extinctions are estimated to be at least one thousand times faster than pre-industrial times.
Soils and arable land	Many regions have lost fertile topsoil. Up to one third of arable soil has been lost globally due to human activities.
Water quantity and quality	70% of water use is for agriculture, and groundwater is becoming depleted in arid regions especially. Where water is more available, there is still significant pollution, for example in areas of urban development and intensive agriculture.
Poverty and income disparities	There has been a general reduction in extreme poverty in recent decades. Still, there are regions which have substantial income inequality. This includes some developed countries.

See Sachs (2015), annual United Nations and Worldwatch Institute updates, and Gore (2007, 2017) for more details.

updates on these very important topics (for example, 2019 UNDP Global Outlook and 2019 UNEP Global Environmental Outlook). Climate change is clearly considered the most important and urgent issue (Gore 2007, 2017). Project Drawdown (Hawken 2017) ranks and details 80 major climate change solutions. The United Nations currently lists <u>17 Major Goals For Sustainable Development</u> (United Nations 2020).

All these publications present massive amounts of data in charts, tables and graphs which can be formidable if not overwhelming for most of us. Matson, Clark and Andersson (2016) acknowledge that sustainable development can be very complex. They demonstrate with several examples how sophisticated systems approaches can be applied to this complexity. Two books by Al Gore are intended to be more accessible. The first <u>An Inconvenient Truth</u> (2007) provides a clear summary of evidence for climate change. It also shows important links to the other key environmental and global issues listed above. The second <u>An Inconvenient Sequel: Truth To Power</u> (2017) provides an update for all these issues, and then outlines actions we can take to "help solve the climate crisis."

Sustainability provides the broader context we need to solve this crisis, and much more. We can approach it in a relatively simple and down to earth fashion by focusing on our lifestyles and direct experiences. We should all be able to quickly appreciate the impacts of human development even without the substantial information listed above. Just step outside your home to see how much the vegetation, wildlife, soils and water flow have changed from historical natural conditions. Then go on a road trip to see how extensive these changes are: mile after mile, from one region to another, and even across the country. Climate change can be hard to experience since the cause is gas molecules that are invisible, the impacts are quite variable both in time and space, and it may be many years before the effects are clear. Still, in regions like California, prolonged droughts and unprecedented wildfires are a very real part of a new normal. One key lesson of the Coronavirus pandemic is that what is not visible to the naked eye, including both greenhouse gases and viruses, can still have devastating impacts. To understand and mitigate these impacts, we need to reach down to the microscopic levels and below. Then we can work on ourselves first, from the inside out, before proceeding to the actions with larger groups listed in Gore's second book (Gore 2017).

There are several important conclusions we can reach after reading the publications above and many others. First, sustainability is a very powerful and vital framework for addressing our most significant issues. Second, sustainability projects and programs can yield significant results. Finally, participation and action by individuals need to be addressed and emphasized more. As part of an excellent summary of sustainability at the time, Edwards (2005) compiled organizational statements of Sustainability Principles from 39 organizations starting in 1978. 28 were international in scope, 9 national, and only one each went down to the regional and local levels.

This final point motivates this book. The main goal here is to focus on sustainability at the individual level in order to improve our personal lives. This provides the most solid foundation for contributing to solutions for the above issues at the larger scales. Given the complexity of global and regional issues, an emphasis on these higher levels can lead to inaction at the individual level. What can one person do about even just one larger issue? Sustainable development projects can involve very large and complex teams even at the local and regional levels. Sustainability is broader and can be scaled down to your level and benefit your lifestyle. This book assumes the reader is concerned about these issues and so is ready to move on to lifestyle solutions detailed in the following chapters. It provides a solid positive and tractable foundation for improving your health and finances. Two key complementary approaches are outlined. First, immense global and very large regional issues are scaled down to the individual level which is most relevant and tractable to act on. Second, positive practices and reasons for adopting a sustainability approach and best practices at the individual level are emphasized. It is easy to be motivated by fear when confronted by intractable global problems. It is much more productive to act on a positive foundation of individual human health, happiness and prosperity which includes social and spiritual, as well as material, dimensions. This book provides a broad foundation for your heart and soul as well as your brain. An abundance of great sustainability examples and practices are presented here. They will improve the quality and length of your life, which is reason enough to adopt them. Many can give you immediate results, and others require more time. All this can in turn contribute to the best solutions at the regional and global scales.

Thus this book emphasizes a grassroots "bottom up" approach to sustainability which has a foundation of individual strength and self-sufficiency. This compares with the "top down" approach which begins with global issues, leaders and institutions. It can provide the physical infrastructure and other resources to further all our efforts. Ideally, these approaches are complementary and can be united with quality communication and two-way interaction between these levels as discussed below.

This book's mission is accomplished when you fully realize the tremendous potential of the sustainability approach to improve your life. With a solid conceptual foundation, it can be applied to changing technology, social and physical circumstances throughout your life. Thus you can reevaluate and make adjustments at all key stages of your life including student, young adult, mid-life, and retirement. The desired results are continuous improvement and personal enrichment (both spiritual and material), as well as contributions to the greater good for other humans and species, now and into the future.

Brief History and Definitions

Sustainability has many important antecedents dating back for centuries (see for example Edwards 2005, Portney 2015 and Brinkman 2016 for detailed historical summaries). The most widely quoted definition is of the Brundtland Commission of the United Nations on March 20, 1987: "sustainable development is development that meets the needs of the present without compromising the ability of future generations to meet their own needs." (see World Commission on Environment and Development 1987). In addition, the following are in Caring for the Earth: A Strategy For Sustainable Living (1991 IUCN/UNEP/WWF): "Sustainability. A characteristic of a process or state that can be maintained indefinitely... Sustainable development. Improving the quality of human life while living within the carrying capacity of supporting ecosystems." Two galvanizing United Nations meetings were the above Brundtland Commission (World Commission on Environment and Development 1987) and the Rio Earth Summit (United Nations Conference on Environment and Development 1992). This stimulated many including myself to participate in international development projects and programs. The focus on development demonstrates the emphasis on the global and regional scales rather than the individual. During the 1990s sustainability finally reached the private sector. Today many large corporations have well established sustainability departments and agendas. These departments have been able to improve operations, the financial bottom line, and corporate communication and responsibility with the public. This presents a much greater opportunity for consumers to demand and support green products.

At the individual level, two phrases that have gained much traction at the consumer level are "go green" and "sustainable lifestyle." They emphasize environmentally friendly products and consumption – "reduce, reuse, recycle." According to Wikipedia, the Go Green Initiative (GGI) was founded in 2002 in Pleasanton, CA by Jill Buck. Since then there have been many "go green" efforts, both public and private. Consumers can find many products labeled "green." While some of these products have certifications such as Green Seal, Energy Star, and USDA Organic, many others do not. So consumers often have to decide how truly "green" a product is. This book helps you make those decisions, and it provides many updated concepts and practices that can improve your lifestyle.

Sustainability has three major pillars: environment, economy and (social) equity (Figure 1.1). These are commonly called the three E's of sustainability. We can

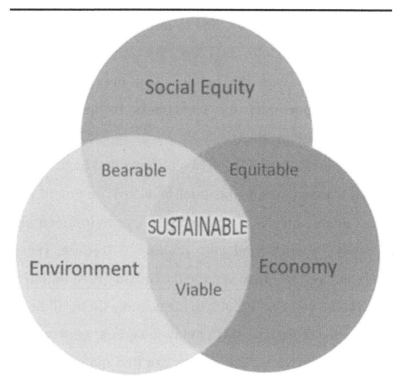

Figure 1.1. The classic three E's of sustainability: environment, economy and social equity. When just two are combined the results can be bearable, equitable or viable. To reach the "sustainable" sweet spot, efforts on all three E's are integrated for the best results.

combine this with the above definitions for the operational definition used in this book: ***Sustainability meets our economic, environmental and social equity needs without compromising the ability of future generations to meet their needs. A balanced integration of these three key elements improves the quality of our lives while keeping within the carrying capacity of supporting ecosystems.*** Figure 1.1 is tremendously powerful because it is a way to visualize how the highest quality sustainability integrates and balances all three Es, rather than emphasizing just one or two as in much work to date. Note that this goes beyond the Brundtland and other definitions above by explicitly including the three Es and demonstrating how they interact. If only two Es are combined, the results are still only bearable, equitable or viable. All three Es are needed to reach the full potential and richness of sustainability.

Music is one way to clarify this point. Music also has three major components: harmony, melody and rhythm. Without all three, or when at least one is off, the music can suffer. The best music integrates and balances the three. There are many wonderful ways to reach this, as demonstrated by the many excellent genres of music. This also applies to sustainability. There is no single "correct" path. Rather, the paths are as diverse as their starting points and approaches are globally. There are many ways to make progress, and we get the best results when all three Es are combined. At the individual level, we can all survive with an emphasis on even just one sphere such as economy or social/equity. This book demonstrates that making the conscious effort to include and balance the additional spheres results in a much more fulfilling and meaningful lifestyle.

Sustainability can and should be a foundation for personal growth and prosperity. For this we need to avoid the limitations of earlier definitions and how they may be interpreted. Here are some limitations which we should overcome. First is the idea that sustainability is a goal with a static endpoint. This does not take into account constantly changing technology, social and environmental conditions. Thus, our goals should be adjusted accordingly over time. Second and related to this is the idea that there is one sustainable "solution" for all. The best solutions are customized for your particular needs and circumstances. This is a great opportunity for you. This book helps you first determine the best solutions for you, and then monitor and make adjustments through time.

Figure 1.2 shows the hierarchical relationships of sustainability at three scales: global, regional and individual. The latter are nested within the former. This is shown by the dotted lines connecting the scales. Note that the placement of the dotted lines can reflect the quality of connections between scales. In this hypothetical case, a very well-balanced individual lifestyle connects and contributes to the sustainability heart of the region (the goal of this book). The region is stronger on economy and environment than social equity, which reflects the reality of many regions. So the connection of this region to the global is farther away from the sustainability heart and contributes more to viability.

Figure 1.3 shows the three Es at the individual level with key areas we can all act on, some even on a daily basis. Like Figure 1.1, it can be tremendously powerful. Striving for integration and balance of these three spheres is how you can derive the most meaning and relevance for your lifestyle. This serves as a guide for your priorities and efforts, which change and evolve with time. They are not static endpoints set in stone. While we should all strive for the greater balance show by the three main circles, we will not necessarily reach the

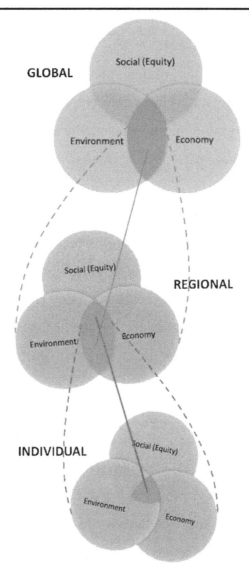

Figure 1.2. The three Es of sustainability at the global, regional and individual levels. In this example, the thick line connects the individual to the heart of regional sustainability (the goal of this book), while the regional need for more social equity contributes more to global viability rather than sustainability.

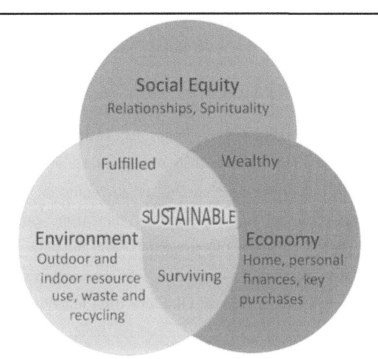

Figure 1.3. Key areas of sustainability at the individual level. Note how this relates to Figure 1.1 at the higher levels.

"sustainability" sweet spot in the middle, which is constantly changing as all the conditions in the three spheres change with time. So the focus should always be on the process of improvement. Figure 1.3 can continually remind you of lifelong priorities, and to reset goals periodically to maintain those priorities. This conceptual foundation with the three E's can be at least as powerful at the individual level as it has been at the higher levels. The following chapters demonstrate that

15

this can add quality and years to your life. This is also the best foundation for contributing to sustainability at larger scales.

Others including Mulligan (2015) and Edwards (2015) have recognized the importance of this individual scale. Mulligan's approach is to replace the economic sphere with "personal." This is an important step towards recognizing this "personal" dimension. Still, I maintain in this book that it is most useful and powerful to keep the three key spheres, with the emphasis on balance between them, at all scales from individual to global. Economy exists at all these levels, and the hierarchical approach allows us to identify and integrate the key parts of the three Es at all levels (Figure 1.2). This provides the opportunity to have much better communication between these key scales so we can integrate individual and grassroots action with leadership, policy and infrastructure at higher levels. Edwards (2015) provides some interesting psychological approaches and perspectives. By comparison, this book emphasizes practical approaches for our consumer choices and lifestyles.

Sustainability: A Many Splendored Thing

Like love, sustainability has become a many splendored thing. What I mean by this is that sustainability can mean very different things to different people including environmentalists, government officials, entrepreneurs and the media. This should not be surprising given that this broad group of stakeholders includes a wide range of backgrounds and priorities. For a given issue such as new housing, a highway or open space, the environmentalist, developer and government official will each emphasize their own interests. They can all sit at the table and disagree while all use the term "sustainability" to defend their position. Many environmentalists are basically concerned with environmental sustainability, just one of the three Es. Many business people and politicians are basically concerned with another of the three Es, economy. Finally, human rights advocates are focused on social equity. This has lead to the term "sustainababble" (Engelman 2013). The key for all these specialists is to appreciate and apply the sustainability definition above fully. While all specialists are partially correct, none are getting the full benefits of a true sustainability perspective and process until they understand and incorporate all three Es, not just one or two.

17

Environmentalists need to consider more than just "environmental sustainability", say in preserving land. Likewise, politicians and businesses that call for "sustainable economic growth" should incorporate wise resource use and environmental quality. The highest quality social equity includes the broadest possible economic prosperity, and the wisest use of natural resources which allows transfer to younger and future generations.

This also applies at the individual level. Figure 1.3 shows the key parts of our lifestyles that correspond to the three Es. Many (if not most) of us are focused and strong in some areas, but neglect other areas. **Surviving** corresponds to *viable* in Figure 1.1. This combines the strength of the economic and environmental spheres. It ensures survival, but at the cost of social relations that enrich us and contribute to the greater good. **Wealthy** corresponds to *equitable* in Figure 1.1. This combines the strength of the economic and social spheres. This is the fastest path to accumulating wealth and sharing it with those closest to you, but at the cost of those farther removed, other species and natural resources, and future generations. This may be the closest to the "default" lifestyle in the United States that is supported by our current technologies, values and media. **Fulfilled** corresponds to *bearable* in Figure 1.1. This is the least selfish, so it can be great psychologically and for our relations, but at the cost of the material well-being and financial stability most of us want.

We can all improve by first recognizing where we are, and then making the effort to combine all three Es more fully. This is an ongoing dynamic process through one's life. Mine is a good example. When I was younger, my environmental and social spheres were strong, but I was also living month to month, especially as a graduate student and through my first job. So then I correctly had to focus more on the economy sphere. However, in hindsight I overcompensated. As my economy sphere became much stronger, the social equity sphere suffered because I spent so much time at work. This book is part of my effort to improve the social equity sphere with stronger and more positive social connections, including you the reader.

This example demonstrates how a sustainability approach can guide and adjust your life plans and priorities. It can help us understand and contend with changes throughout our lives. You will get the greatest benefit by using this book interactively. This begins with being aware of the areas you want and/or need to improve. So let's first evaluate where you are now, and then determine how you can improve additional areas. Figure 1.3 and Table 1.2 show the key parts of a sustainable lifestyle. Note how Figure 1.3 corresponds to Figure 1.1 for the global and regional scales. Social relationships includes family, close friends, neighbors and community (including volunteering), and work.

Table 1.2. Key components of a self-assessment for a sustainable lifestyle. Five key factors are listed for each of the three Es. First rate yourself for each factor. Then add up the factors for each E (maximum score of 10). You can then plot these three summary scores on Figure 1.4A for your sustainable lifestyle profile.

Social (Equity)	Economy	Environmental
0-2: Family	0-2: No Debts	0-2: Renewable Energy Use
0-2: Friends	0-2: Net Income	0-2: Home Energy
0-2: Work	0-2: Savings	0-2: Transportation Energy
0-2: Community	0-2: Investments	0-2: Water Use
0-2: Spiritual	0-2: Contributions	0-2: Outdoor Activities

Spirituality can be with or without a religious institution. Economy includes personal finances including income, debts, savings, investments and contributions. It can also include ownership of sustainable products at home and for transportation. Finally, environment includes practices that use clean energy sources and reduce pollution, conserve energy and water, and maintain a healthy and pleasing environment.

We can visualize and even quantify and rate our lifestyles along axes for each of the three Es (Figure 1.4). A very sustainable lifestyle (lighter) has high scores on all three major axes, for a relatively small area. A much less sustainable lifestyle (darker) has lower scores, for a much larger area. Figure 1.5 compares two more hypothetical examples: a younger person that scores highest on the social equity axis vs. an older person that has a higher score on the economic axis. Using these figures as a guide, is your lifestyle centered on one of the Es, or where just two overlap (survival, wealth, or fulfillment)? Do a self-assessment using the criteria listed in Table 1.2. You will have a score of up to 10 for each of the three Es. You can then graph your lifestyle to identify where you are on Figure 1.4A. This is your starting point today.

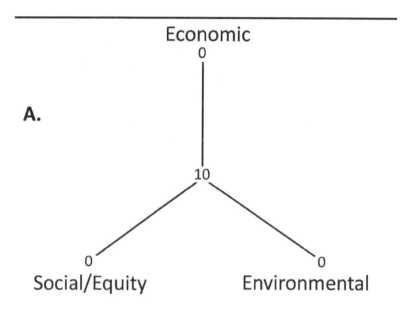

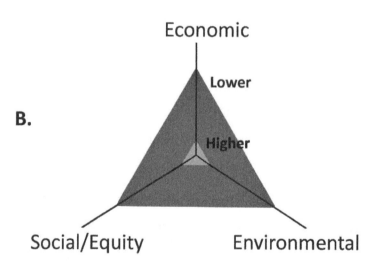

Figure 1.4. A. The three Es of sustainability, with each axis ranging from zero at the ends to ten in the middle. B. A comparison of high (light) and low (dark) sustainability lifestyles.

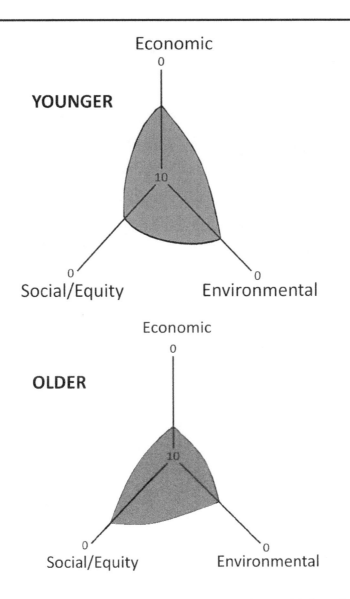

Figure 1.5. A comparison of two hypothetical lifestyles: younger with higher social equity score, and older with higher economy score.

You can then set priorities and goals as you read the following chapters. We can all strive to improve our consumer decisions for key needs including food, water, housing and mobility. These chapters detail updated approaches and techniques for each of these key parts of our lives. As you read these chapters, note the steps you can take towards sustainability. At the end of each chapter, there is a page available for you to list and organize actions ranging from daily and easy to more time consuming and long term. At the conclusion, you can bring together all these actions for a self-assessment of these goals. It may be best to do this first for daily and easy actions, and then for longer term projects. Rate how much they will improve your scores for each of the three axes. You can then have much clearer goals and visualize how they are helping you reach a more sustainable lifestyle.

Personal vs. Individual

While preparing this book, I replaced "individual" in the title with "personal". This reflects my effort to make the subject as meaningful as possible for you. Emphasizing "personal", I invite you to take a deep dive into the spiritual, psychological and ethical dimensions in

Chapters 2 and 3. While much of this is at your "individual" level, it is also much deeper and thus personal. This is also about being able to connect with others in a more positive and profound manner after taking this deep dive. "Individual" can mean you alone, which we must go beyond. While the sustainability practices in this book can lead to more self-sufficiency, we must also ultimately work with others to address the larger issues which impact our individual sustainability journeys.

Overview

Following this introduction, we focus on the personal level in two chapters: the first on spirituality (Chapter 2), and the second on goals and aspirations that drive all of us (Chapter 3). These are subjects that are not even mentioned in much sustainability literature, perhaps because they can be so deeply personal. That is precisely why these topics are presented here, so you can address your deepest motivations. They are profoundly important to reaching sustainability goals since there are long held assumptions and practices that need to be updated. Sustainability concepts and practices are ideally suited for this. Chapter 3 presents a new American (and Global) Dream that is informed by the sustainability perspective. The outdated American Dream focused on material wants and needs. The sustainable American Dream is abundant spiritually and socially as well as materially.

We then emphasize the power we can have as consumers in Chapter 4. Wise and informed consumer decisions fully leverage that power, and this can create the demand for more and better sustainable products. With clean renewable energy sources and recycling, we can have more rather than less consumption, which can offset the more wasteful and polluting alternatives. Then we go to the two keys for our survival and material well being: food (Chapter 5) and water (Chapter 6). For food, much has already been written about nutrition and growing healthy food. This is summarized, and this chapter also focuses on how you can best access healthy food that also supports the local economy. This includes regional farm to fork efforts, buying locally, and growing your own food. Water is an increasingly precious resource, especially in states like California. Thus individual needs and consumption patterns are reviewed to point the way toward improvements.

We then move on to key technological developments for the two most significant expenses of most consumers: housing and transportation. Both can now be powered affordably and reliably by renewable energy sources including solar and wind. I have found that many consumers need to understand the energy units (especially kWh) and terminology for these energy sources and uses. Thus Chapter 7 is a primer for consumer electricity use and needs. Then energy uses for both homes (Chapter 8) and mobility (Chapter 9) are discussed, with an emphasis on recent improvements including solar, batteries, and plug-in electric vehicles.

The above two chapters demonstrate that the technology already exists for greatly improved sustainability. There are still barriers to the adoption of these technologies that are deeply imbedded in our biology. These barriers are addressed in a chapter on sexuality and population (Chapter 10). Finally, Chapter 11 concludes with a summary and integration of the above chapters. You can use this to set lifestyle priorities and connect with the larger community and bioregion. This overview provides the foundation and context for the sustainability adventures in this book. The following

three chapters provide strong and practical motivations
to begin your journey at a personal level.

———

Chapter Two

MODERN SPIRITUALITY AND SUSTAINABILITY

———————

Most of this book provides a foundation for more sustainable lifestyles with solid scientific numbers and facts. We all make decisions based also on our beliefs, values and emotions. Thus a critical part of our personal journey is to go deeply within to understand and improve our innermost motivations. This gives us a better attitude and perspective for applying the information and technologies presented in the later chapters to our lifestyles. All this greatly enhances our sustainability efforts. Sustainability can enhance spirituality, so this is a great place to start.

Spirituality focuses on the "deepest values and meanings by which people live" and centers on the "spirit as opposed to material or physical things" (see for example Wikipedia Definition). Sustainability adds environmental and social dimensions to the economic (material) dimension which is central for most of us. The social dimension connects us to other humans, however different they may be. The environmental dimension connects us to other living beings and the resources we depend on. So these dimensions have great potential for taking us beyond narrow material goals and striving for larger goals with more spiritual meaning. This is profoundly important and should have a significant impact on our individual decisions and actions. Perhaps because this can be profoundly personal, it has not received much attention in texts on sustainability and sustainable development. The closest they come is some mention of ethics (for example Chapter 12 in Theis and Tomkin 2015). I distinguish spirituality (a core part of our being) from ethics (moral principles which are constructs of individuals or groups). While ethics can provide useful guidelines, especially in a workplace and organizational setting, they are not necessarily deep and personal. Thus the emphasis here is on spirituality rather than ethics.

Spirituality can be a key means to making sustainability more effective and meaningful. In turn, our sustainability journeys can help us to overcome the shortcomings of religious institutions. One key shortcoming is that most of these institutions were not created to embrace the tremendous ethnic and cultural diversity we now have in countries such as the USA. Instead they continue to have the ethnocentric values and beliefs of where and when they originated. The sustainability foundation of social equity can overcome this (Figure 2.1). A second key shortcoming is religious

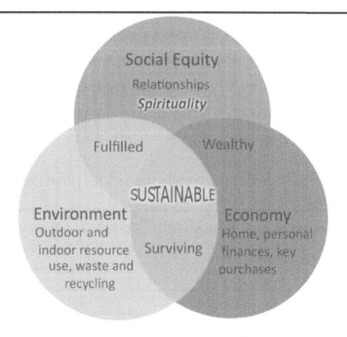

Figure 2.1. The three Es of sustainability at the individual level. Note spirituality is within the upper sphere.

doctrine based on outdated historical information rather than science and current verifiable facts. This doctrine may have been based on the best intentions and information of the time, but it still needs to be updated and reconciled with what is available today. Sustainability has a scientific foundation which includes environment/resources, so it is well positioned to meet our modern needs. This is the opportunity for institutions that want to be modern and relevant, and for individuals who want to develop spiritually.

How can sustainability become vital for meeting our modern spiritual needs? For many of us, these needs are not being met by religious institutions. In the USA, fewer people are going to church and subscribe to a given institution (Table 2.1). The main reason cited is that

Table 2.1. Spirituality trends in the USA (Pew Research Center 2017 and Wikipedia).

Most Of Us Are Religious	54-74% and declining
Fewer Actually Attend Church	20% and declining
Most Of Us Are Spiritual	75 %
Spiritual But Not Religious	28% and increasing

religious institutions do not reflect their beliefs and values because they have become outdated (see also Maher 2008 - Religulous). They helped many cope with the hardships of life hundreds to thousands of years ago. However, they have not been updated sufficiently for modern educated people which aspire to a higher and more sustainable standard of living. This is made clear by many recent surveys and trends. Currently, most people in the USA still consider themselves religious, but the percentage is declining to 54% (Pew Research Center 2017). This includes about 74% Christian in 2015, down from about 85% in 1990 (Religion In The United States Wikipedia). Active participation in religious activities is even lower. Only about 40% state they attend church regularly, and this percentage has declined even further to 36% recently. This is one clear signal that religious institutions are becoming less relevant, and another is that actual attendance at church is estimated to be closer to 20%. This has led to publications including Why Nobody Wants To Go To Church Anymore (Schultz and Schultz 2013).

Most people in the USA also consider themselves spiritual (75 percent according to Pew Research Center (2017)). One very significant trend is the percentage of those who consider themselves spiritual but not religious. While historically it has been at about 20%, it has grown to about 28% in about five years (Pew Research Center 2017). Another estimate for this growing group is even higher at 37% (Wikipedia "spiritual but not religious"). It is also notable that the greatest increases (10-13%) are for younger (teens to 40s) and more educated people (at least some college education). All this confirms that our spiritual needs are not being met by religious institutions. So this is our opportunity to develop a spirituality made more relevant and contemporary by sustainability.

There are two major ways we as individuals can integrate sustainability into our spirituality. First, since most of us are affiliated to at least some degree with a religious institution, we can work within that institution. Gore (1992) emphasizes how compatible this is with Judeo-Christian tradition generally (p. 243), and specifically with many Christian groups and practices. Second, there are many opportunities outside of these institutions for the growing number of "spiritual but not religious." Finally, we can all try some combination of the two. Here are some of the options.

We can begin with the vast network of institutions in operation. These religious institutions can become updated and more relevant by adopting sustainability practices. John Carroll makes the case that spirituality can contribute to a strong foundation for a sustainable lifestyle in his 2004 book <u>Sustainability and Spirituality</u>. He lists "five outstanding examples of spiritually-driven and faith-based community models" in the United States: Sacred Heart Monastery in North Dakota, Tierra Madre in New Mexico, Heartland Farm in Kansas, Prairiewoods in Iowa, and Michaela Farm in Indiana. Notably, they continue to have strong spiritual foundations grounded in their religious identification. In addition, over the years they have developed sustainability practices suited especially for their locations including clean energy sources, housing materials, and crops cultivated. A second more recent update on this topic is <u>Spirituality and Sustainability</u> (Dhiman and Marquez 2016).

Most of us do not have the time or inclination to be part of intentional spiritual communities. Still, there is much we can do to help improve the religious group we are affiliated with. Steve McSwain has written several blogs which summarize key problems and solutions for religious institutions (<u>McSwain Huffington Post Blogs</u>).

The first lists their current challenges and shortcomings: demographic remapping (less White, and older), technology, leadership crises, competition, (more) religious pluralism, "contemporary" worship experience, phony advertising. The second and third blogs list his key solutions. I summarize most here (in bold) with some editing, and then add my commentary to demonstrate how sustainability can contribute to these solutions.

- **Embrace change**: sustainability can fuel positive and relevant change by balancing an individual's economic concerns with social equity (love thy neighbor, and support cultural diversity) and the environment (our resources, and the eternal) in a long-term multigenerational context.

- **Appreciate growing diversity within (and outside) the Church**: McSwain shows here and in the third point how fundamentalists within a given Church can divide, reduce and possibly even destroy that Church. I would add that we should all support and appreciate even broader diversity to include non-Christian groups (Buddhist, Hindu, Muslim, etc.). Sustainability can help provide that broad nondenominational foundation.

- **Make friends, instead of enemies, with people who disagree:** while this is considered a Christian virtue, fundamentalists especially do not subscribe to this virtue. This point and the two above and below are the best tests for what a given Church is about. The more ideologically, culturally and politically rigid, the more it is about power and resources for its leaders. On the other hand, the more open a Church is to our growing diversity of backgrounds and perspectives, the greater opportunity to serve a given individual's spiritual needs and growth. Sustainability is broadly nondenominational, so it can certainly contribute.

- **Stop using the Bible and worship to mask prejudice or promote a political agenda**: these are signs of outdated Churches that do not serve a diverse public. Sustainability at its best has a strong all-inclusive foundation which should resist narrow political agendas (see also Chapter 11).

- **End the war on science, biology, and psychology**: this is a key area where sustainability can provide a solid and updated foundation since it is based on science and fact (see Chapters 1, 4-11). The significance of this point cannot be overemphasized.

The sooner we can all appreciate facts and scientific processes, the sooner we can pull out of cultural and economic crises toward a more sustainable future.

- **It's time for a new or revised Christian theology**: sustainability can help provide the conceptual foundation that makes a new or revised theology more meaningful for our present-day needs.

- **The Church is declining, but God is not dying**: this relates to what is most significant for all of us at a deeply personal level. While outdated Churches are declining, our spiritual needs remain strong. That is the opportunity for new principles and practices. The time is right for sustainability to contribute to a more modern and relevant spirituality.

Here are some large institutional programs that individuals can connect and contribute to through their Churches:

- **Green Faith** is an Interfaith organization that includes both Christian and non-Christian denominations. It has programs including certifications for both houses of worship and individuals: GreenFaith

- **Creation Justice** Ministries includes a broad range of Christian organizations: CreationJustice

This is just a small sample. Edwards (2015) discusses many faith-based programs including Interfaith Power & Light. Blumberg (2014) provides a large listing of 15 organizations: Religious Environmental Organizations

In addition, we can develop spiritually independently of religious institutions by working directly on sustainability practices. Here is a list of activities and practices that can be very spiritual (see also above references):

- **Nature and outdoors:** for many, outdoor activities including hikes can be remarkable spiritual experiences. Ecological and nature-based belief systems include Wicca, Shamanic, Druid, Gaia, and Native American (see also Gore 1992, p. 258). Many natural features can provide deep spiritual fulfillment and connections even without these systems. For me, this includes redwoods towering over us that have lived hundreds of years, geological formations such as the Grand Canyon which took millions of years to form, and the sheer beauty of features such as Lake Tahoe. All these are humbling and provide connections to the eternal which are beyond words. Perlmutter and Perlmutter (2020) provide an update of the many substantial health benefits of spending time in nature (see their Chapter 6 "It's Not Man Versus Nature – Getting Back To Our Roots").

- **Music**: for some this can be the basis, not just a part, of their spirituality. Like nature, music can go beyond words to bring out our deep spiritual feelings. There is some great common ground between music and sustainability in enhancing one's spirituality. Music also has three major components, which are harmony, melody and rhythm. Without all three the music can suffer, and the best music integrates and balances the three. There are many wonderful ways to reach this, as demonstrated by the many excellent genres of music. This is how both music and sustainability can enhance one's spirituality. They can both help navigate life's complexities with beauty, flexibility and balance.

The above outdoor settings and music can be combined with eastern influences such as Zen and meditation (for example mindfulness, transcendental), and physical activities including Tai Chi and Yoga.

All of the above can meet our deep spiritual needs by connecting us to what is much larger and eternal. This can be much more meaningful than the words and stories of organized religions which may be outdated and otherwise not relevant for our modern lives. These activities go well beyond words to the core of our emotions and consciousness. Our dreams and aspirations can also reside this deeply, so that is the subject of the next chapter.

Spirituality – My Actions Toward Sustainability

Daily:

Short Term:

Long Term:

Chapter Three

A GREATER AMERICAN (AND GLOBAL) DREAM

———

The first two chapters have shown how sustainability can improve us personally and spiritually. This chapter continues this theme with the dreams and aspirations that deeply motivate all of us. We all have dreams and goals that are very specific to our circumstances. Still, one cannot deny the impact of what is broadcast to us on a daily basis through the news, film, sports, music, internet and other media. This chapter recognizes that the American Dream is communicated and promoted through all these media for an enormous impact on our beliefs and actions. Thus, I begin with a brief historical overview and assessment of the current American Dream. This allows us to identify key strengths and weaknesses. Then I demonstrate how sustainability can update and improve our American Dream, and how we as individuals can immediately put this into use.

Brief History and The Current American Dream

While roots can be traced to our Declaration of Independence, the term "American Dream" is credited to Adams (1931): "life should be better and richer and fuller for everyone, with opportunity for each according to ability or achievement" (see also American Dream in Wikipedia). It is important to appreciate this historical context. During the 18th and 19th centuries this dream was very much associated with our western frontier. More land and resources were always available for those willing to conquer and develop them. So, an American Dream which focused on the individual's ability to work hard served many generations quite well. Immense regions of wilderness have been converted to lands that provide a range of economic benefits. There are two key outcomes. First, material wealth is the key metric of success. Second, there is an emphasis on the individual's ability to succeed (win) in the face of enormous physical challenges. These are both logical results of countless efforts in frontier environments.

The American Dream has served us well during the expansion and growth of over two centuries. Now for it to serve us well in the coming decades and centuries, it needs to be revised and updated. We can now place less emphasis on material wealth, especially when it conflicts with our overall quality of life. Our frontiers are no longer physical. They are more cultural, technological and mental. We need to update and improve the American Dream to meet these new needs. The conceptual foundation for sustainability is ideally suited for this. In Figure 3.1 the larger Economy sphere represents the American Dream emphasis on material wealth. By comparison, an updated Sustainability Dream has Environment and Social spheres that are the same size as Economy (Figure 1.3). This reflects greater balance and integration, centered on sustainability rather than economy.

Celebrity and The American Dream

This is where we can see most clearly the current state of the American Dream, and how it can be improved for all of us. Sternheimer (2015) provides an interesting account of the changing relationship between celebrity and the American Dream during the past

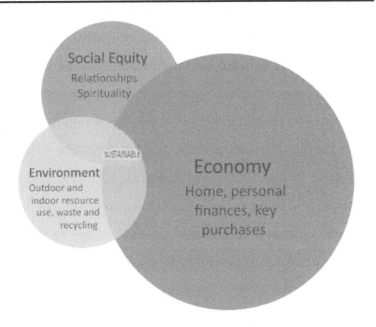

Figure 3.1. The three Es of sustainability at the individual level for the Americal Dream (note larger Economy sphere).

century. Two key constants over time are the focus on material wealth as the key sign of success, and that this apparent success does not necessarily lead to a long and happy life. Professional football is particularly relevant since it is a very physical sport that reflects the American ideal of fighting through pain to reach success. These are the unfortunate results for NFL athletes. Despite high earnings while playing, the vast majority (up to 80%) have financial difficulties within 2 years of retirement, and many enter bankruptcy within 5 years. They live much shorter lives (55 years), many with serious lifelong injuries. Mez et al. (2017) found that of 111 former NFL football players, all but one (99%) were diagnosed with CTE (chronic traumatic encephalopathy)! The vast majority also had behavioral, mood and cognitive symptoms, and signs of dementia. While few of us face the challenges and perils of the professional football field, we can all be driven to excess in pursuit of the American Dream. This can take the form of overworking, abusive and/or neglecting relationships, and substance abuse. Sustainability can help by balancing the emphasis on material wealth with elements which lead to long and happy lives including strong social connections and a balance of the material with the spiritual.

The California Dream

The California Dream can serve as a bridge between the American Dream and a new improved Sustainability Dream. The appeal of California is clearly demonstrated in the media and songs such as "California Dreamin'" by the Mamas and Papas. Another song is "Go West" originally by the Village People and then popularized by the Pet Shop Boys which includes these lyrics:

(Go West) Life is peaceful there

(Go West) In the open air

(Go West) Where the skies are blue

(Together) We will love the beach

(Together) We will learn and teach

(Together) Change our pace of life

(Together) We will work and strive

(Go West) This is our destiny

My first days in California one December many years ago quickly confirmed the warm and sunny weather compared to the eastern United States. Starr (2005) points to something much deeper:

"California has long since become one of the prisms through which the American people, for better and for worse, could glimpse their future. It had also become not the exclusive, but a compelling way for this future to be brought into existence."

In this excellent detailed history, he describes how the 1849 California Gold Rush became the quintessential example of the American Dream. Ordinary people who made the effort had the opportunity to get rich quick. The reality was much more brutal for most, with many physical and mental challenges. Still, a global reputation was established as the land of opportunity.

Since then, several factors have maintained this to the present. First are the abundant natural resources and features. Resources include soils and climate for world-leading agriculture, mining, timber, and now renewables including solar, wind and hydro. Features include Yosemite, Lake Tahoe, the redwoods, and a spectacular coastline. Add to this the "California state of mind", supported by tremendous cultural diversity, which provides a freedom and entrepreneurial spirit to collaborate and try new things. A key part of this is an emphasis on science and technology to create new economic opportunities.

In September 2019 I attended a gathering at a country ranch where Gavin Newsom spoke to a diverse group about the California Dream (Figure 3.2). He emphasized how the California Dream is special because of the many factors listed above. Then he listed the key roadblocks to broader access to this Dream: widening income inequality and less affordability (especially housing). So, while there is much to be proud of in California, much more progress is still needed especially in Social Equity, the third key pillar of sustainability.

Figure 3.2. The author (second right) with Governor Gavin Newsom (second left) and others after the Governor spoke about the California Dream Sept. 2019.

All these factors point to the key elements that can sustain a new and improved Dream for all of us. First, develop the broad collaboration needed to promote inclusion and equity. Second, use natural resources wisely, and focus more on renewables to the extent possible. Finally, through education and research, develop scientific and technological tools to bring all this together for new opportunities. California has spectacular examples of how this can work including agricultural productivity, media, entertainment and high tech. Still, it also reveals what we need to overcome. The cost of living, especially housing, is too high, especially for those working in urban areas. Related to this are widening income disparities. Environmental challenges include air pollution, fires, water shortages and loss of soil fertility. So, while California is pointing the way to solutions, we still need to go beyond what has been accomplished in this state.

Toward A Sustainability Dream

These are key ways that sustainability can improve and update the American and California dreams for our modern needs:

- First, it can correct the emphasis on material wealth as the main goal of the American Dream. As the above examples clearly demonstrate, wealth by no means assures a long and happy life. This needs to be balanced by priorities on healthy relationships, spirituality, diet and exercise which a sustainable lifestyle supports. A goal of abundance which has mental and social, as well as material, dimensions can replace the prevailing wealth paradigm (see also Edwards 2015).

- It includes the foundation of social equity. We can all view this as an opportunity to build respectful and productive relationships as broadly as possible in our increasingly diverse communities. This helps us appreciate the strength of diversity so we can build on it. One can argue that the United States is the best global example of opportunity for all, and we certainly have made much progress. However, we cannot deny that historically certain groups and regions have not shared the same opportunity. So, leveling this playing field with genuine respect for all ethnic and cultural backgrounds needs to be a focal point for moving forward.

- Referring to the original Adams (1931) definition of the American Dream, the three Es of sustainability add "better" and "fuller" to a "richer" life. In addition, they are totally compatible with the concept of upward mobility. Indeed, they enhance it by providing the foundation for extending upward mobility to future generations.

Make America (And The World) The Greatest Ever

In moving forward, it is important to resist being too nostalgic about the past since there is so much that can and should be done to improve our present and future. We can certainly be proud of our remarkable heritage. For example, I am a Son of the American Revolution with ancestors dating back to the eighteenth century in the Boston area, and at least one who fought in the American Revolution. Still, I appreciate that over the centuries the opportunities were greatest for white Christian families in certain regions. Even so, many still endured hardships we should try to eliminate for all. On my father's side, some relatives had to endure the working conditions of West Virginia coal mines. Occupational medical conditions included black lung. So, I certainly do not want to wane nostalgic about this, and instead want to support much better work and living conditions.

I emphasize this point because there is always a temptation to view the past with rose-colored glasses. "Rosy retrospection" is a psychological condition in which the past is recalled and judged disproportionally more positively than the present. Many including myself readily recall positive events and feelings, while forgetting past hardships and inequities. This could help explain some of our current cultural and political debates. For example, the phrase "Let's Make America Great Again" first used by Ronald Reagan in 1980, and then slightly rephrased and popularized by Donald Trump, implies that America was once greater than now, so we should somehow recapture that America. Look more carefully and we find that America has been great for only a subset of the population which is now shrinking, and even for that subset outdated technologies and industries no longer apply. So, it is not simply unproductive, it can actually be dangerous to be nostalgic about a great America. Instead, we need to look clearly and realistically to the future. What are the best available technologies for using our precious resources wisely? And how can we make our increasing diversity a fuel for growth?

Values

A sustainability perspective can improve both our spirituality and aspirations. Here is a summary of how our values and priorities can be strengthened so we can make opportunities out of challenges:

- Understand, appreciate and promote diversity. This ranges from material (e.g. food, biodiversity) to social (ethnic and cultural) to spiritual (faith-based and otherwise).
- Embrace change with social, technological and other tools. Resilience can help mitigate negative impacts of change.

- Shift from the prevailing paradigm of material wealth to one of abundance which gives equal value to non-material wealth including mental and physical health, and better relationships.
- Shift also to "green" consumption as detailed in the next chapter.

After I wrote the first draft of this chapter, I came upon an effort that is remarkably relevant to this chapter and leads to the next. New Dream (formerly Center for a New American Dream) is a nonprofit organization which has an overall goal to, ". . .reduce consumption, build community, and improve quality of life." It focuses on the individual and community levels. They conclude that the New Dream must be based on new attitudes towards wealth, consumption and consumerism. This final topic is the subject of the next chapter.

Dream – My Actions Toward Sustainability

Daily:

Short Term:

Long Term:

Chapter Four

POWER OF THE SUSTAINABLE CONSUMER

This chapter emphasizes the impacts you can have while improving your lifestyle as a consumer. In the USA, consumer spending has been nearly 70% of gross domestic product (GDP) during the past decade (U.S. Bureau of Economic Analysis 2020), and the global average has been 57-58% during the same period (World Bank 2020). Per capita consumer spending in the USA was $36,966 in 2017 according to World Bank Data. You can view this as the average annual amount each of us can spend more sustainably. The consumer decisions we make every day can strengthen sustainable practices, support sustainable products, and thus improve our lives and communities (see also Portney 2015). One promising trend is that in the USA younger millennials are more likely to buy sustainable or socially conscious brands (75%) compared to older baby boomers (34%)

(Nielsen 2018: <u>Sustainability Landscape</u>). A growing number of sales trends globally reflect our efforts to be both "healthy for me" and "healthy for the world", which brings us closer to the sustainability sweet spot (Figure 1.3).

The most obvious and conventional approach to reducing our environmental impacts is to consume less. Simply, if you can reduce consumption by 50%, you can reduce your impact and costs by the same amount. This can slow the rise of "hyperconsumption" (Mulligan 2015). This can be applied especially to large upper-income McMansions (also called Millennium Mansions) which can be designed for excessive consumption and waste. Still, there are cases in lower income communities especially where the greater need is for more access to and consumption of healthier products. Prime examples are food "deserts", usually in urban disadvantaged communities, where healthy fresh food is not available. Generally, we need to advocate and financially support greener products so they are at least as easy to choose as traditional products.

So, in this chapter I emphasize this complementary alternative to less consumption: purchase and use of products that are healthier and have a much lower carbon and broader environmental footprint. As the following chapters demonstrate, these "greener" products can be great improvements. If you can reduce your impact to 10-20% without reducing consumption, you are still well ahead of the 50% above. In addition, you are financially supporting the greener product so it can eventually replace or at least be a significant alternative to inefficient and wasteful products.

This alternative approach is also compatible with the concept of abundance. It proactively supports products that are based on renewable energy sources with rapidly improving cradle-to-cradle designs (Matson, Clark and Anderson 2016). The basic idea in these designs is to eliminate waste with recycling. What could be waste streams destined for landfills are instead converted to the raw materials for new products. When this is powered by renewable energy, we can all support abundance sustainably. This is more appealing to mainstream consumers compared to limiting or reducing consumption. While cradle-to-cradle design is by no means feasible for all products across the board, remarkable progress has and will be made when manufacturing efforts are guided by these goals. Our consumer demand and dollars can hasten these efforts.

It is key to recognize that currently much, if not most, of our consumption is based on marketing and convenience rather than the best information and choices. This can lead to unhealthy food choices, poor resource use, inefficient homes and transportation. Many wasteful and unhealthy products have reached an economy of scale that is hard for the individual and larger economies to resist because they are the least expensive and most convenient. However, these are generally just short-term benefits. Cheap processed foods can have enormous long-term health costs. The current childhood obesity epidemic is an example of how significant the impact can be even early in life. Many other cheap products deplete soils and water, and they may use nonrenewable energy sources. So, while they are expedient, they can be much more costly over years to decades, and for future generations.

We can all contribute to climate change solutions when we understand and reduce the major impacts of the products we use on our carbon footprints. Recent estimates for our per capita greenhouse gas (GHG) emissions in the USA are 16-20 tons per year. To meet the Paris accord goal by 2050, we must reduce to 2.1, and the current global average is 4.5. There is enormous variability in both the total amount and major sources geographically: over 100 for Wyoming, under 10 for New York, and only 0.47 for Bangladesh (Worldometer CO2

Emissions). The proportion of the major factor in the USA, animal products, can vary 18-51%. Still, the key factors are covered in the coming chapters: food, materials and energy used in products we purchase, especially our homes and mobility. The Center For Sustainable Systems, University of Michigan (2020) lists several carbon footprint calculators so you can estimate your footprint and take steps to improve your score.

So, it is critical for us as consumers to be better informed, and then be able to make the decision to purchase the best products available. "Going green" is now part of the marketing of many companies, and how "green" a product is can vary tremendously. Some companies claiming to be "green" may have products and practices that can still be improved substantially. "Greenwashing" refers to misleading or even false information about the environmental benefits of a given product. On the other hand, there are small local businesses that truly are quite "green" and sustainable without the resources to advertise and market these benefits. So, we should all take the time to find the available local resources, and network with other consumers to support the best "green" businesses.

One way to sort out truly "green" products and businesses is to look for certifications. Currently there are over 20 certifications available for a broad range of products, and I highlight four of the best known and most respected. Figure 4.1 shows their labels which can be used only after meeting certain criteria. Here are brief summaries, with website links to detailed criteria and standards:

🖉 **USDA Organic:**

https://www.ams.usda.gov/services/organic-certification

This certifies that a farm or handling facility meets the USDA standards for "organic" for crops, livestock, processed products, and wild crops.

🖉 **Energy Star:**

https://www.energystar.gov/products?s=mega

This provides ratings for a broad range of appliances, lighting and other electronic equipment. The Energy Star is awarded to products that can significantly reduce energy use without sacrificing performance.

🖉 **Green Seal:**

http://www.greenseal.org/GreenLiving.aspx

This non-profit organization certifies a very broad range of products. Standards are listed for each category.

🖉 **LEED:**

https://new.usgbc.org/leed

Leadership in Energy and Environmental Design

certifies buildings at levels which include Certified (40-49 points), Silver, Gold, and Platinum (80+ points). Thus, consumers can support businesses and workplaces with these certifications.

Organic

LEED

EnergyStar

Green Seal Certified

Figure 4.1. Major certification labels for green products.

This is what I have learned over many years both as a consumer that tries to be green and as a business person selling green products:

First, be aware that each and every purchase can support more sustainable products and lifestyles. This is the undeniable power we all have. Even our smaller daily purchases including food quickly add up over time. And the "big ticket" items such as housing and transportation are also especially critical. At the time of purchase, or in the short term, a greener product may be more expensive. However, it may prove to be less expensive over the years if it is more reliable, uses less energy and has lower maintenance costs. Certain long-term costs including air quality/health, water quality and soil fertility can be impossible to estimate accurately, so this is another reason to pay more for a greener product at time of purchase. It is also smart to support the local and regional businesses that make the extra effort to provide green products and also contribute back to the community.

Second, take the time to be informed about local and regional resources. These vary tremendously according to where you live. So, a good starting point is to look for the above certifications and labels that can be found throughout the USA and other countries. Then you can look more closely where you live. You may find some businesses with exaggerated or incomplete "green" claims. Hopefully, you will also find some "diamonds in the rough" – local businesses which are quite green without advertising the fact. Finally, you can encourage a business to become more sustainable by requesting greener and better products, services and facilities, and then support those improvements with your consumer dollar.

Some recent ideas and terms for more sustainable products include sustainable luxury, slow food and slow fashion. **Sustainable luxury**: for some this may seem an oxymoron or contradiction since luxury can be associated with excess and waste. However, there is also a common ground we can support: products that are high-quality, durable and reliable. They do not go out of fashion, and can last an entire lifetime. Especially if they are made with the right materials and labor practices, there is definitely a place for sustainable luxury. Two more terms are part of the **Slow Movement** which emphasizes quality over expediency (Honore 2004 –*In Praise Of Slow*). **Slow food**: this term refers to a movement that promotes local food and cultures. The Slow Food Foundation was founded in 1989 and is discussed in more detail in the Food chapter. **Slow fashion**: this emphasizes quality, longevity, and sustainable materials and practices. It is both inspired by and parallels slow food (Fletcher 2007). It also overlaps significantly with sustainable luxury.

In summary, this chapter provides a balanced and positive perspective on consumerism. There has been much emphasis on "less consumerism" and a "minimalist" approach that reduces clutter and nonessential items. All this is well taken. Still, we as living entities are by definition consumers. There is no way to avoid at least some consumption. Our daily acts can support more sustainable materials, practices and ultimately a healthier economy. In addition, we can have a positive impact on the economy by choosing and using more sustainable products as they become available through time. Theoretically there is no limit to sustainable consumption that uses clean renewable energy and materials, and includes complete recycling of non-renewables. Ideally, we will reach the point that these products are so prevalent that they become the foundation for our lifestyles and thus our economy. The next two chapters address how we can start with what is most fundamental to our daily consumption: food and water.

Sustainable Consumer – My Actions Toward Sustainability

Daily:

Short Term:

Long Term:

Chapter Five

FOOD

———————

Food is the first of four key parts of a sustainable lifestyle in this book since it is so central to our survival and health. Our food choices can have the greatest impact on our carbon footprint (Project Drawdown 2017, University of Michigan 2018, Foer 2019). Agriculture has been key to the sustainability movement because it can be an excellent example of how wise resource use leads to tremendous economic, environmental and social benefits. Food can be more than our source of nutrition. It can also be one major way to maintain our key natural resources, in particular soils, water quality and quantity, and biodiversity including forests, plant and animal species.

Thus, this chapter focuses on food choices we can make to both improve our diets and support these larger systems. It emphasizes first the best food choices for you, and then outlines the many ways you can access those choices conveniently. This goes beyond a reductionist "nutritionism" which simply views food as the sum of its individual nutrient components. We first need to appreciate how all these nutrients interact with any additives and supplements to affect our bodily health. Then we also need to understand the impacts of fresh local sources versus larger-scale agribusiness. Thus, your food choices at both these levels can contribute to your community, environment and economy as well as to your bodily health.

Improving Your Current Diet

A good starting point is to assess and understand your diet in relation to USA national averages. For this, we can go to the 2015-2020 Dietary Guidelines For Americans. It includes a summary of current nutrition patterns and needs for improvement:

Current Eating Patterns In The United States

Figure 5.1A shows that we are eating too many processed foods that can lead to our obesity epidemic. We are also not eating enough fresh fruits and vegetables (Figure 5.1B). Per capita food consumption in the United States

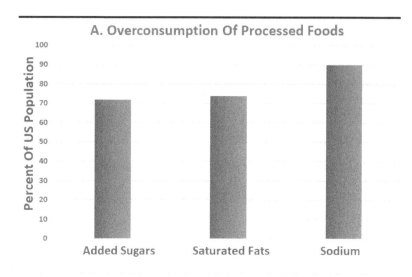

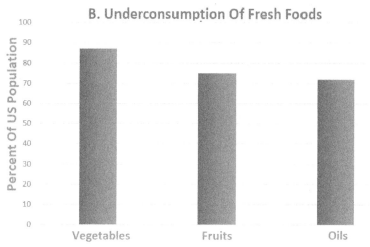

Figure 5.1. The US diet in relation to recommendations. A.) shows the percent of the US population that is consuming over the recommended limit of added sugars, saturated fats and sodium. B.) shows the percentage of the US population that is eating less than the recommended level of fresh vegetables, fruits and oils. Based on data from **What We Eat in America, 2015-2020 Dietary Guidelines For Americans** (U.S. Department of Health and Human Services and U.S. Department of Agriculture 2015).

is about 5 pounds per day. The United States Department of Agriculture recommends that we consume at least 2000 to 2500 calories per day. The right amount depends on factors including weight, activity level and age. Actual consumption is over 3700 calories, well over these recommendations. This is still well below production capacity since the United States is the top exporter of food to other countries. There is also plenty left to waste. One estimate is that we waste 1249 calories per capita per day (NPR 2014).

Figure 5.1 illustrates some remarkable key eating patterns. First, most people in the United States eat well over the recommended levels of added sugars, saturated fats and sodium (Figure 5.1A). This is clearly due to the high amounts of processed foods and red meat we consume. Associated with this is high caloric intake which leads to over two thirds of US adults being overweight or obese. Second, and just as clear and striking, at least three-fourths of the US population eats less than the recommended levels of vegetables, fruits and oils (Figure 5.1B). You can compare your eating patterns to recommendations to see how healthy your current diet is, and how it compares with others in the USA.

This figure is an excellent example for a major point in the last chapter on consumption. Clearly in the US we are overconsuming packaged and processed foods high in calories. We are also not eating enough fresh vegetables, fruits and other nutrient-dense foods. So, we need to go beyond the simple notion of consuming less. Instead, we need to focus on shifting our consumption patterns and habits to healthier alternatives. Thus, most of this chapter is dedicated to this.

It is useful to note some major food trends. The above US dietary guidelines are based on a massive and growing WWEIA (What We Eat In America) data base which was started in 2001. Bowman et al. (2018) compared 2003-2004 vs. 2015-2016, so they were able to find statistically significant trends. Here are some key results:

- There has been a significant reduction in added sugars from 21 teaspoon equivalents to 16.2 teaspoon equivalents daily per person. Unfortunately, this lower amount is still too high. Also, some of the low-calorie artificial sweeteners which have helped bring this level down have their own health concerns (see below).
- A significant reduction in the intake of solid fats.

- An increase in consumption of whole grains is slight but still significant. The per capita consumption is still below the Dietary Guideline recommendations.

All of these positive trends are due to greater awareness and availability of healthier food choices at grocery stores and restaurants. This is what we can build on. Still, there is clearly a need for much more progress. Perhaps the strongest case for this is that Bowman et al. (2018) did not find any significant changes for fruits and vegetables, so their consumption remains below recommended levels.

The above studies and recommendations emphasize the clear benefits of eating locally grown fresh food in favor of foods that are highly processed and refined with preservatives and other additives. Several recent PBS (Public Broadcasting Service) health specials take us one step further. They demonstrate that fresh nutritious foods have benefits well beyond weight control and physical health. They are also vital for cognitive abilities, mental health and the best aging. Many of the ideas presented by Joel Fuhrman, Mark Hyman and David Perlmutter in these specials are also in the following books. Fuhrman (2011) advocates a "nutritarian" diet of fresh unprocessed foods rich in nutrients. He documents how this can solve major health and longevity challenges including obesity, heart disease and diabetes. Hyman (2018) provides an excellent summary of the best food choices based on the most updated scientific information. He emphasizes the benefits of whole fresh foods that can be recognized as such. Perlmutter and Perlmutter (2020) provide compelling updated information on how foods affect brain function, mood and behavior.

Here are some key ideas for improving your food choices and diet based on updated information:

- **Plant vs. animal foods**: The benefits of a diet lower in animal products has long been appreciated and promoted. My sister introduced me to two related books shortly after they were published. Lappe (1971) and Ewald (1973) demonstrated how much more food is available when we eat lower on the food chain. They also focused on the concept of protein complementarity to improve plant-based nutrition. Both books have great recipes which my sister and I enthusiastically tried (see also below). Since then there has been growing concern about both the nutritional content of meats and the resources and additives needed for livestock. Hyman (2018) states that at the nutritional level meat is better than previously thought. Foer (2019) takes into account the many costs of production and impacts on climate change to make the case for less meat. Project Drawdown (2017) provides detailed analyses to support this.

One concern about vegetarian and vegan diets is that they can be bland. I have found that meatless alternatives can be at least as tasty and nutritious using recipes in the above books and by now many others. Meatless burgers are another example of great alternatives. I have also learned to appreciate the convenience and versatility of salads. They are easy to prepare, and the combinations of ingredients and seasonings are limitless.

Sustainability Adventure 1

Better Foods. _One great experience I had as a college student was the introduction of Ewald's (1973) meatless lasagna and other vegetarian dishes to the cafeteria food in a "Better Foods" evening. My freshman class was required to eat at the cafeteria which at the time (mid 1970s) served the typical institutional food high in fats, sugars, and additives, packaged rather than fresh. I was among many who were missing home cooking, so I could easily have led a student protest which was also quite typical those days. Instead, I chose to focus on positive solutions. I selected nutritious recipes that I knew_

---

tasted great, and then coordinated with cafeteria staff to scale up these recipes to preparations for hundreds of students. The result was a celebration rather than a protest. The student response was overwhelmingly positive, and most thought the taste was at least as good as with meat. This event lead to permanent improvements towards fresher and more nutritious meals at all cafeteria locations. This is what you can do with the many ideas and practices presented throughout this book. First try them to find what works best for you. Then scale up and share especially what works best and you enjoy. I had prepared the vegetarian lasagna recipe several times with family and friends before trying it for hundreds of students.

- **Sugars and carbohydrates:** There is overwhelming evidence including the studies listed above that most of us need to reduce our intake of both sugars and carbohydrates, especially when they are processed, preserved and packaged. Perlmutter and Perlmutter (2020) demonstrate how these foods can cause poor decision making and depression. Disconnection Syndrome caused by these inflammatory foods is due to the shift of favorable activities including empathy, centered in the pre-frontal cortex to more primitive functions of the amygdala in the limbic system which includes impulsiveness, narcissism, and self-centeredness.

- **Vitamins and supplements:** It can be overwhelming to see how many pills and powders claim to improve your diet and health. The consensus of medical and nutritional professionals is that we can and should get our key vitamins from nutritious foods without resorting to supplements. Fuhrman (2011) is an excellent guide for how you can do this.

There are two major concerns for how many foods are produced and packaged for the consumer. First are the pesticides, hormones, additives and other chemicals used to produce many plant and animal foods. Second, evidence is also mounting for the harmful effects of toxics/plastics used in containers and packaging. Phthalates is one example. Currently there are many more chemicals in use compared to what can be monitored (one estimate is 8000 vs. 300). Thus, their synergistic and cumulative effects cannot be determined. All the more reason to favour foods that eliminate or at least minimize these two major concerns.

Getting and Supporting Local Food

All the above confirms how important it is for us to get local fresh foods. So how can we do this conveniently? Many of us already have access to thriving regional agriculture we can support. I am blessed to live in a region that is ideally suited for growing and buying fresh food. The Central Valley of California is the source of most fresh produce for much of the USA as well as California. With neighboring regions, it also provides the majority of almonds and certain types of rice for global markets. Thus, Sacramento has been proclaimed the Farm-To-Fork Capital. This effort links regional consumers to the rich variety of local food sources. Their annual festival gives consumers the opportunity to meet local farmers and see what they grow. They can also sample and purchase these products from the grocery stores, markets and restaurants which emphasize these local sources.

This is one way for the consumer to start learning about regional resources, and fortunately this is increasingly available throughout the country. The term Farm-To-Table is also used. The key for the consumer is getting the food conveniently and reliably at a reasonable cost. Here are some key options, starting with the easiest:

- Grocery stores: now even major chains feature local and organic foods. This is a great way to support these sources since your decision will encourage the large mainstream chains to stock and continue selling these items. These fresher choices are usually on the perimeter of the store, so shop there first before going to the interior aisles with more processed and packaged foods.
- Direct shipment to your home. I have a local organic farm group ship to me every four weeks. I make the final selection online about a week before shipment, and it is delivered to my door.
- Coops, health food stores and other specialty stores for larger quantities, supplements and other specialty items.
- Farmers markets bring local farmers closer to you on a weekly or other regular interval.
- Farm-To-Fork restaurants. In the Sacramento region, Produce Express is a distributor which links regional farms to restaurants.
- Special regional programs such as "Double Up" created by Fair Food Network. This targets underserved communities, providing participants an additional dollar for every dollar spent on fresh fruits

and vegetables. It originated in Michigan and has grown to over 25 states.

Sustainability Adventure 2

__Andean potatoes.__ The conventional potato is unremarkable: brown skin, white and watery inside, and a bland flavor without seasonings. During the late 1970s I participated in a project which demonstrated to me how remarkably interesting potatoes are in their Andean cradle of domestication (Brush, Carney and Huaman 1981, Carney 1980). We documented how Andean farmers maintain a great diversity of potatoes. This includes shapes, colors and patterns (Figure 5.2), textures, nutrition and taste. Since then I have come to appreciate that there are many examples of this for a broad range of vegetables, fruits and other crops throughout the world. For most of us, this includes at least a few near where we live which deserve our support. We can also support farms which maintain soils and wildlife in our regions. One prominent example in my region is the Rominger farms.

Figure 5.2. *Andean potato diversity (photo of International Potato Center).*

The **Slow Food** movement promotes local foods and cultures. The slow food foundation was founded in 1989 (www.slowfood.com). It has expanded to over 150 countries, including Slow Food USA. The main goal is to promote "good, clean and fair food."

There are also more options for growing food on your own, or in your neighborhood. One positive trend during Coronavirus is that more people are devoting time to their gardens while staying at home. Here are some of the options, starting with the simplest at home:

- Fruit trees and herbs.
- Hydroponics and other indoor grows.

- Small home plots, intensive raised beds, on up to enough cultivation to be self-sufficient on your own land! See for example urban homesteading by Jules Dervaes and others (Anger et al. 2015).
- Neighborhood gardens and orchards. These can be maintained by your HOA (Homeowners Association) as well as residents. One example in northern California is Village Homes, where residents can use certain community garden areas, and staff maintain orchards which residents can harvest.
- Regional community gardens.

In summary, the goal is to choose what works best for you to secure a healthier diet while also supporting a stronger local economy, healthier soils and better water use. Many of our food choices are changing rapidly, and this creates opportunities for us. Amanda Little provides an interesting and very readable summary in The Fate Of Food (2019). Here is a summary of some of the promising ideas and technologies that we can consider and support:

- *Aeroponics* and other related indoor grow and greenhouse techniques. Aeroponics can greatly reduce the need for arable land, water, pesticides and fertilizers with indoor "vertical" farming. Some locations near urban centers can already provide lettuce and leafy greens (which otherwise spoil rapidly) to grocery stores and restaurants quickly and reliably. The growing periods can be 12-16 days, for up to 25-30 harvests annually. With the many improvements in materials and LED lighting (see also later chapters), these facilities can be very energy-efficient with renewable sources. At the home level, personal food computers (PFCs) are being developed which can be programmed to grow specific crops such as herbs, tomatoes or peppers. The "climate recipe" provides the light, temperature, water and nutrients for what you want to grow.

- *Aquaculture* as a critical source of protein and other nutrients. The growth in aquaculture has been hailed as a "Blue Revolution." Coastal salmon farms have grown to the size that there are concerns about environmental impacts. Freshwater species grown in a broad range of systems include carp, catfish and tilapia. At the base of the food chain there is farming of algae that ranges from enormous coastal kelps to microscopic Spirulina (a source of omega-3 fatty acids as well as high-quality protein). All these products are increasingly available at grocery stores.

- *Meat alternatives* which can range from plant-based to cell cultures. Plant-based alternatives have been available for many years, and there is a broad range of opinions about their quality. One recent improvement for many meat lovers is the inclusion of plant heme (blood), which makes products like the "impossible" burger look and taste more like meat burgers. Another alternative is cellular meats cultured and grown indoors. This can tremendously reduce waste (no body parts), time, energy and water use.

- *Nutritious foods* which can be cultivated in hotter and drier conditions with poorer soils. There are already many foods available which can help us adjust to changing climate conditions. One notable example is quinoa which can grow with both less water and more saline, poorer soils. It is already available as a key ingredient in many foods including entrees, salads and bars. Moringa is a plant that does well in hot dry climates, but still needs work to become more edible.

- *Meal-replacement alternatives* which range from drinks to preparations from 3-D printers. This includes preparations such as Soylent and many "survivalist" and emergency foods that can last from months to years. There is concern that these cannot provide the quality nutrition of fresh organic foods.

Still, they are a relatively nutritious alternative to conventional fast foods. Thus, they can be a good option when you do not have the time for preparation.

Food – My Actions Toward Sustainability

Daily:

Short Term:

Long Term:

Chapter Six

WATER

————

L ike food, water is critical for our survival and a more sustainable lifestyle. In arid regions such as northern Africa and the United States southwest, water is the limiting resource that dictates both development (where can people live, and how many) and agriculture (what crops, and in what quantities). Higher temperatures caused by climate change increase even more the demand for already scarce water resources in many regions (Gore 2017). Globally, at least one in 10 people lack access to safe water supply (Postel 2013). Women and children in developing countries walk a daily average of 3.7 miles and carry 5 gallons of water to their homes (Sakakeeny 2019, Postel 2013). In developed countries such as the USA, most of us are fortunate to have much quicker access to running water. That also means it is much easier to use and waste much more water. This can lead to larger regional problems including groundwater depletion, soil erosion and salinization, pollution and less water for others.

Water is one of the best examples of the many ways we can reduce use without reducing quality of life. In fact, conserving water may even improve our quality of life and help us develop more appreciation for this precious resource. This chapter summarizes individual water needs and uses. It begins with what our individual minimum needs are, and then reviews the major sources of our per capita water uses. Significant improvements can be identified by simply going through this process. This provides a foundation for evaluating and improving your water uses.

Minimum Needs

First, we can establish what you need for survival. For many years the recommendation has been to drink at least one-half gallon (64 ounces, about 8 glasses) per day. This is also known as the "8X8" rule. More recent recommendations are 91 ounces for women and 125 ounces for men (Institute of Medicine 2004). Factors which can affect the right amount for a given individual include weight, exercise, extreme heat or cold, and health condition. Thus, an active male may need closer to one gallon per day, while a female that weighs much less may need closer to one half gallon. We obviously have other daily needs including cleaning and food preparation. Still, this information makes it clear that one's minimum water needs can be just a few gallons per day.

For drinking water, we should pay attention to quality as well as quantity. In the United States most of us are fortunate to have drinkable water available at the tap. In 2016, over 90% of local water systems met federal standards according to the Environmental Protection Agency (EPA) (Drinking Water In United States). Most that do not are small and rural, so the larger urban systems are generally considered safe. You should be able to receive annual Consumer Confidence Reports (see EPA above, and EWG below) from your water provider which reports on water quality, including sources and contaminant levels. One important comparison to EPA federal standards is the EWG (Environmental Working Group) tap water database (see https://www.ewg.org for 2019 update). You can conveniently access information about your drinking water by entering your zip code. They have found that 81% of US water systems have contaminants liked to cancer (this includes hexavalent chromium for 77% of us). For over 160 contaminants, the federal government has not set limits.

So EWG has set standards based on available scientific information for these contaminants. Their limits are also generally much lower than federal levels which have been set to date. My water district is a typical example: 13 contaminants exceed EWG guidelines. Of these 7 are below the federal legal limit, and 6 have no legal limit. Now you can look up your water supplier to see how your drinking water compares.

EWG advocates substantial reductions of these contaminants as long-term solutions. Meanwhile, they emphasize home filtration. This can also take care of contaminants in the plumbing leading to your taps. Water filtration at your home can remove chlorine and impurities, but it can also remove beneficial minerals such as calcium and magnesium. Filters can also get contaminated, so if you have one you want to keep it clean. There is a broad range of opinions on the benefits of filters. This is due to substantial differences in water quality according to location, and types of filters. Thus, you want to make a decision based on your particular circumstances. EWG lists three major types of filters: activated carbon, reverse osmosis, and ion exchange. Carbon is the least expensive, while reverse osmosis is generally most effective (especially when combined with carbon filter).

Plastic water bottles have become ubiquitous. While occasional use in public is understandable and convenient, there are concerns about regular use including at home. According to EWG (2019), bottled water can cost about 2000 times more than tap water (at least a dollar per gallon compared to 2 cents per gallon). Second, the quality is generally no better, and bottled water may have additional contaminants which do not have to be disclosed. The plastic in the bottles can add many contaminants, and only about one third of bottles are recycled. Finally, it has been estimated that the energy needed to produce and ship bottled water can be up to 2000 times as much as for tap water.

Actual Use

Now we can go on to the total amount of water that we typically use. Per capita water use in the United States can average 80 to 100 gallons per day according to USGS: Home Water Use). WECalc (http://wecalc.org/calc/#) has higher estimates of 69 gallons/day of indoor use and much greater 235 gallons/day for outdoor lawn and plant use per person! Figure 6.1 is a pie diagram that shows the major types of outdoor and indoor water uses. Here are the key uses and ways to improve them:

Water Use

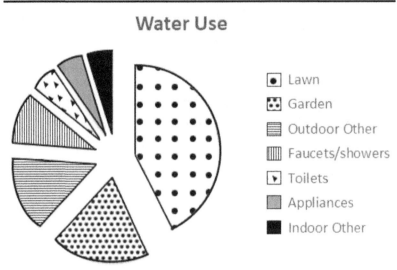

Figure 6.1. United States national average daily water use per person. The major uses are approximations from several sources, and the actual amounts can vary greatly by household and region.

- Lawn and garden can account for the vast majority of household water use. Thus, practices such as xeric landscapes (Figure 6.2), better sprinklers and drip irrigation, and ET (evapotranspiration) sensors can have tremendous benefits.

- Low-flow faucets and showerheads can reduce major indoor uses by over 50 percent.

- Newer toilets can reduce water use from 3-4 gallons/flush to 1.6 gallons/flush.

Figure 6.2. Two examples of xeric landscaping. In the first, small lava rocks replace grass lawn, and in the second wood chips are used. Both feature a broad range of beautiful drought-tolerant plants. This practice alone can reduce home water use by over 50%.

- EnergyStar dishwashers and clothes washers can save lots of water and electricity. New dishwashers can use less water than hand washing.

Individual and household water use can vary tremendously depending on the region you live in, and household size. One excellent tool for evaluating your water use is WECalc (http://wecalc.org/calc/#).

I did this for my home, and it confirmed that outdoor lawn and garden are generally at least 60% of my total water use. I have worked with my local water district, Sacramento Suburban Water District (SSWD), to reduce this use. I began with a water audit and simple improvements. The total use can now fall below 50 gallons/day during the wet season when I turn off sprinklers and irrigation, but then the daily use can climb to over 100 gallons during the hot and dry summer months. This is even after replacing the back lawn with xeric landscaping, improving sprinkler heads and drip irrigation, and installing an ET sensor. Thus, converting the front lawn to xeric also will reduce my water use the most. My major indoor water uses are faucets, toilets and showers. I am well below the national average of 69 gallons per day because I have low-flow faucets and showerheads, newer toilets and efficient washing appliances.

Local and Regional Water Quality

In regions that receive higher rainfall and other sources of water, we should emphasize maintaining quality of this precious resource. Fertilizers, pesticides, household toxics and debris can cause downstream pollution and affect wildlife. Erosion from your property affects soil as well as water quality. So here are some of the things we can do:

- *Hazardous materials* do not pour used motor oil, anti-freeze, paint and other toxic fluids down household or storm drains. Coordinate with your waste management service for best disposal.
- *Fertilizers, herbicides, pesticides* reduce or eliminate use of fertilizers (especially nitrogen and phosphorus), herbicides and pesticides. All of these can be toxic for downstream wildlife.
- *Scoop the poop* cleaning up after pets reduces levels of potentially harmful nutrients and bacteria in waterways.
- *Erosion, runoff* these can be reduced or eliminated in many ways. Bare spots can be eliminated with

xeric and other landscaping. Low-lying areas can include "rain gardens", wetlands and other features that filter and retain runoff. You can even make driveways, walkways and other features more permeable to reduce runoff to the nearest storm drain.

- *Clean up* the waterway nearest you. This can start with simply picking up litter. Creeks, rivers, ponds and lakes can all be restored from eyesores to beautiful and healthy attractions for all. Community projects can be a great way to work with neighbors to create and maintain special places. Ideally, these projects integrate our enjoyment and use with vital functions for regional water quality and wildlife.

__Sustainability Adventure 3__

__Water.__ I've been blessed to have many aquatic adventures both in the USA and globally, small lakes to large lakes to oceans. Perhaps the most beautiful was Lake Tahoe (Figure 6.3), where I contributed to the program to "Keep Tahoe Blue."

Figure 6.3. Lake Tahoe. Source: Heath Carney.

In Latin America, I discovered and helped describe a major species new to science (Cyclotella andina Theriot, Carney and Richerson 1985) and also helped document the benefits of native raised bed agricultural practices for both water quality and farmer yields in the highlands of Peru and Bolivia (Carney et al 1993, Carney, Kozloff and Cook 1994). Taken together, these adventures have demonstrated to me how water is beautiful and fascinating, as well as vital. Recognizing this, our human practices can ingeniously use, adjust to, and preserve our aquatic resources wherever we live.

In summary, our current per capita water use is clearly well over our basic needs. The good news is that there can be dramatic improvements with little impact on, or even better, quality of life. Indoors, there can be dramatic improvements with newer faucet and shower heads, toilets and washing appliances, even while maintaining the same water use habits. Outdoor uses for lawns and gardens are the greatest, and they are also some of the easiest to improve with better equipment and nighttime watering. Converting lawns to more xeric alternatives can be quite interesting and also reduce maintenance in the long term. Many of my neighbors have made these alternatives an opportunity to make their homes more unique and beautiful compared to those with conventional green lawns (Figure 6.2). This is a remarkably positive example of our capacity for resilience. Most of the xeric projects in my neighborhood began a few years ago during the drought years when we all had to reduce our water use. Many came up with a solution that is lower maintenance, more appealing and thus increases home value. In areas with greater rainfall, low maintenance alternatives with natural vegetation for that region can be very attractive alternatives to lawns. This can reduce the need for costly equipment, fertilizers and pesticides as well as maintenance time.

Water – My Actions Toward Sustainability

Daily:

Short Term:

Long Term:

Chapter Seven

kWh: NEW COIN OF REALM FOR CLEAN ENERGY

———————

With this chapter we shift from the basics of daily life to the tremendous opportunity we have to improve our modern lifestyles through electrification with clean energy. Some of the most notable recent progress toward sustainable living in recent years has been the vast improvements in clean energy technologies and infrastructure. The technologies for capturing, storing and using solar, wind and other renewables are improving every year in performance, reliability and cost. For example, the costs of solar photovoltaic panels have declined substantially in recent decades. Costs of renewables continue to go down annually relative to fossil fuels (Figure 7.1). Solar and wind energy costs have declined dramatically in the last ten years and are now even lower than natural gas. Coal has been relatively stable at more than twice the cost, and nuclear has become the most expensive major source. Most of new solar and wind power during the coming decade will be less expensive than fossil fuels (Dudley 2019).

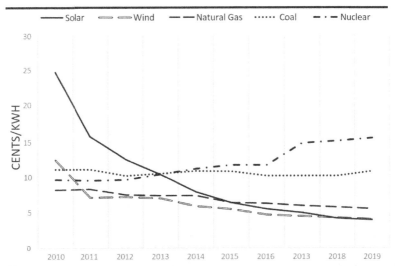

Figure 7.1. Global costs of renewable and other major energy sources at the utility scale during the past ten years. This is based on much more detailed analyses and data in Lazard (2019).

With this, many products are becoming available that can use these renewable energies more efficiently and at lower costs. At home this includes air and water heating, air conditioning, LED lighting, and use of all appliances. For mobility this includes not just a car for commuting, but also your other major transportation options including scooters, buses, trains, boats and even airplanes. Electrification of all of these is becoming more practical every year for the same reasons. Costs of conventional transportation fuels including gasoline continue to climb while renewable sources become much more affordable. Electric motors are very reliable and durable, with fewer parts to replace. Batteries are improving rapidly in capacity, reliability and cost. This provides the opportunity for much more affordable energy storage that is key to stabilizing the energy from solar and wind.

I fortunately live in a region where infrastructure has developed to the point that a consumer can conveniently choose renewable energy sources. In northern California, large wind turbines have been placed in high-wind areas. Solar has expanded rapidly in the last decade, ranging from residential rooftop to larger commercial to utility-scale farms. Even without their own rooftop solar, utility customers can choose to use renewables, such as the Greenergy program of SMUD (Sacramento Municipal Utility District). Key uses including home and transportation are finally affordable and reliable for the consumer. There are now many public charging stations for smartphones, computers, other appliances and vehicles. Increasingly they make sense even without subsidies, especially when you consider use over time rather than just the upfront cost.

I have found that a significant barrier to greater adoption of these promising technologies is that many of us are not familiar and comfortable with the basic units of electricity including Watt, kW and kWh. For many years I simply paid my utility bill without concern about the details. I was only concerned when the bill seemed unusually high. Like many others (if not most), I could not answer basic questions about my utility bills: what was the monthly and daily use in kWh, and what was being charged for that use? I finally became much more interested when I started using home electricity rather than gasoline for my plug-in electric vehicle. This alone saved me over one hundred dollars per month. Installation of rooftop solar also added to my interest and familiarity with basic electrical units. Unfortunately, some utility bills do not provide this information clearly. I am blessed to get utility bills which clearly state monthly use in kWh, amounts charged with time of use, proportional solar generation, and credits for solar and electric vehicle use. However, I have also seen much more confusing bills from other utilities.

Beyond the home, another growing example is car buyers who historically have been fine just understanding miles per gallon (mpg) for fuel efficiency. Thus, they do not know how far an electric vehicle can go with the battery size expressed in kWh, or the amounts needed for refueling. One effort to bridge this gap has been to provide an MPGe (miles per gallon equivalent) estimate for an electric vehicle model. Unfortunately, this can only be a rough estimate based on conversion factors that can vary considerably. To really understand and appreciate key aspects of this technology including fuel efficiency, range, refueling costs and time, it is best to use the electrical terms defined below.

These units are vital because they allow us to communicate what we need and what these technologies can provide. They can be used for all parts of the process including generation, storage, and the major home and transportation uses. The good news is that the fundamental electrical terms are simple, and they cover the whole range of clean energy needs and uses. So, they are listed and reviewed here to provide a solid foundation for you. Then in the following two chapters these units will be put into use for our key energy uses at home and for mobility. The key units to begin with are Watt, kW and kWh (Table 7.1). Watt and kilowatt are

Table 7.1. Key measurements and units of electricity.

W (Watt) [†]	is the key measurement of instantaneous electrical power. For example, many conventional bulbs are 40-100 watts, whereas a 15-watt LED bulb draws only 15 watts at a given moment.
kW (kilowatt)	is 1000 watts. Thus larger home uses are expressed with this unit.
kWh (kilowatt hour)	**is the energy use of one kW for 1 hour. This unit is especially significant because it is used by utilities and others to measure and charge for energy use.** 1 kWh = 3.4 kBTU (kilo British thermal unit – also commonly used for energy use).
1 MWh (Megawatt hour)	1MWh = 1000 kWh, and 1 **GWh** (gigawatt hour) = 1000 MWWh
Ampere (A, or Amp) [î]	is a measure of current of one coulomb per second. Total house amperage can be 100-200 amps. Typical circuits range from 15 amps at 120 volts to 30-40 amps at 240 volts.
Volt (V)	is a measure of the difference in electric potential energy between two points per unit of charge. The standard voltage in the United States is 120 volts for typical outlets, and certain ones including washer/dryer, electric vehicle charger and solar can be set to 240 V. Many other countries, including in Europe, have a standard of 220-240 V.

† Watt has a simple relation to two other electrical units that have widespread use:
î 1 Watt = 1 Volt x 1 Ampere

terms for instantaneous electrical power. kWh (kilowatt hour) is the energy use of one kW for 1 hour. This unit is especially important because it is used by utilities and others to measure and charge for electrical energy use.

Another very common unit which is also used for natural gas and other energy is the kBTU. Fortunately, the conversion between these two units is quite simple: one kWh equals 3.4 kBTU. One useful exercise to become comfortable with these units is to find the wattage for items you use including bulbs, smartphones, refrigerator and microwave. Most bulbs are clearly labeled. Conventional ones are usually 40-100W. LED (light-emitting diode) bulbs can be much lower wattage for the same light intensity. Many people have put LED in locations used the most. Over the years I have been replacing my older conventional bulbs in less used areas when they burn out and can be replaced with LED. Here are some additional daily uses: 2-6 watts for smartphone charging, 100-200 watts for refrigerators (older ones can use much more than newer ones), and at least 700 to 1000 watts for microwave ovens (depending on your power setting).

I Sing the Body Electric

To better understand and appreciate energy use, it is interesting to estimate the daily energy uses of our bodies. We can do this by converting calories to the above terms for electricity. As stated in the food chapter

(5), one recommendation is to eat at least 2000-2500 calories per day, and most of us eat well over that. The conversion of nutritional calories to kWh is 859.65 calories equals one kWh. Thus, if you assume daily use of 3000 calories per day (roughly my average use), that equals about 3.5 kWh. A typical bicycle workout is about 300 calories in 30 minutes, or about 0.35 kWh (350 Wh). This is more than enough to power many smaller devices and appliances. For example, smartphones generally need 6-10 Wh to fully charge, and laptop computers may need about 40 Wh. Major uses such as heating/air conditioning and cars generally need much more energy daily as described in the following chapters.

Two important examples demonstrate the significance and use of kWh. Home and transportation are generally the two major purchases and expenses for a consumer. First, for the home simply look at your monthly electricity bill. You should be able to find your total monthly usage and how much you are charged per kWh (as above, the clarity of utility bills can vary greatly according to the provider). The average household use in the United States is about 1200 kWh/month, or about 40 kWh/day (see Chapter 8). How does your use compare? For transportation, the average daily commute is 29 miles/day (see Chapter 9). An electric vehicle can average about 3.5 miles/kWh. Thus, the average need is about 8.3 kWh/day for those using a full electric vehicle. How does your vehicle use compare? In the following two chapters we will break down this monthly amount down to the key uses at home and with your vehicle. We will also look at how solar and other renewables can contribute to these needs. kWh is the key unit we can use for all these estimates and comparisons.

————

Chapter Eight

HOME

————————

The key opportunities for using clean energy are where we live and work. Most of us spend the majority of our time (including sleep) in our home environments. This is even more the case at the time of this writing during coronavirus. Thus, this chapter focuses on total energy use at the household and individual levels. For our major energy uses, our impacts can range from minor daily adjustments to major long-term improvements. With this information we can identify key areas where we can save energy, and also where we can convert more fully to cleaner energy sources. In keeping with the theme of abundance in earlier chapters, we should note that the energy potentially available from clean renewable sources (including solar, wind, hydro and geothermal) is much greater than our needs. So, harnessing and using them cost effectively and responsibly (minimizing impacts) is key to sustainability.

The average US home has 2-3 people and uses 900-1500 kWh/month, or about 30-50 kWh/day (https://www.eia.gov/tools/faqs/faq.php?id=97&t=3). Per capita use can vary tremendously according to geographical region (how much air conditioning and heating are needed), level of technology use, and how much major uses are shared with others. For example, a one-bedroom apartment can use 500 kWh/month, or 16.7 kWh/day. These values can be lower when there is shared use, and in regions with more moderate climates.

Within the household, these are the major uses (Figure 8.1):

- Space heating and/or cooling. This is clearly the top energy use, and the specific needs vary tremendously by region. Southern regions may not need heating, even in the winter, but they do have high air conditioning needs. Northern and coastal regions may have lower air conditioning needs, but they do have much greater heating needs. For all these regions the best materials and insulation are critical for maintaining the desired temperature. The latest technology in air conditioners, furnaces and heat pumps is also important. One major opportunity is

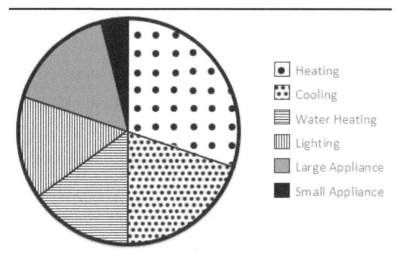

Figure 8.1. Major household energy uses. These are general approximations from several sources. These major uses are consistent for most US households, but the specific proportions and kWh usage can vary tremendously.

to change from natural gas and other fossil fuels to renewable electricity. For example, in my California region this can include replacing natural gas furnaces and water heaters with electric heat pumps for both air and water heating. Heat pumps can be much more efficient and thus less expensive especially in moderate climates (without extended periods of subfreezing temperatures). This is because they move rather than generate heat. There are many types and constant improvements, so they can be increasingly better alternatives even in colder regions. Excellent examples are **geothermal heat pump systems** which take advantage of the relatively constant temperatures underground throughout the year, and the relatively high specific heat of soils and fluids compared to air. Thus, they are efficient even in areas where there are substantial fluctuations from winter cold to summer heat. The heat pumps for these systems connect either to a vertical system of fluid-filled pipes (water with some antifreeze) which can penetrate to a depth of several hundred feet (similar to a water well), or to a shallow and extensive horizontal loop system buried only a few feet under the surface. My brother installed a vertical closed-loop system which serves for both heating during the winter and cooling during the summer. This system saves about $4000 per year compared to the previous heating oil costs. This is without increasing the annual cost of electricity because of the increased efficiency of air conditioning. Within a few years, these savings paid for the cost of installing the system. The savings are even more dramatic with new construction because the true cost of installing such a system is only the net extra cost over a standard system.

- Devices like Nest thermostats can also help us set temperatures that are efficient and comfortable. Without these devices, many of us select very strong air conditioning the summer, and likewise strong heating in the winter which may be a higher temperature setting than in the summer! My per capita energy use is substantially lower than the above averages in part because I set my summertime cooling (say about 80) to much higher than my wintertime heating (say about 70 or even lower). They are both quite comfortable when I adjust layers of clothing to the season. Nest thermostats help make these adjustments quite convenient.

- Water heating. This can be a relatively high energy use with lots of waste during hot water storage that many are unaware of. Thus, setting this up correctly with good equipment that is well insulated, and then following up with good maintenance, is important. Then there is much that you can do to use hot water effectively without waste. This includes setting cooler temperatures on the clothes washer and dishwasher, and limiting shower duration with water-saving flow settings. There are also increasingly attractive alternatives to traditional water heaters including heat pump and/or tankless demand type water heaters. The latter do not store hot water, but rather run cold water over a heating coil that is activated when hot water is demanded through a tap or appliance. Like geothermal heating systems, the initial costs of these systems are higher, but these additional costs can be recouped in only a few years through energy savings.

- Lighting. This is another major use that can be made much more efficient with the latest technology. LED (light-emitting diode) can provide the same light level at a much lower wattage than conventional incandescent or fluorescent bulbs. Thus, bulbs at the 60 to 100-watt range can be replaced by 10-20-watt LEDs. This alone can reduce lighting costs substantially, and motion sensors can also reduce the number of lights left on without use. For exterior lighting, self-sufficient units with portable solar-charged batteries can meet most if not all of your night-time needs.

- Larger appliances. The two larger appliances that normally use the most energy are clothes dryers (especially) and clothes washers. Thus, alternatives to machine drying and washing, and using the temperature settings, can save quite a bit of energy.

Other larger appliances include the refrigerator/freezer, oven and dishwasher.

- Smaller appliances. These include TV/DVD, desk and laptop computers, and phones. They generally use relatively little energy due to their low wattage, but this can add up if they are constantly left on. "Vampire" use can be minimized by using energy-saving standby modes, and simply turning them off when not in use.

In summary, while the above are the major uses for most homes, the proportions and total amounts vary considerably according to location, home size and technologies, etc. Thus, to identify your key energy demands and potential improvements it is best to start with a home assessment. At the national level, the Energy Star program has a great tool:

https://www.energystar.gov/campaign/assessYourHome

Your utility may have programs more specifically suited to your home and location. For example, I am within the service area of SMUD (Sacramento Municipal Utility District) which has a Home Performance Program that includes both a comprehensive review and an upgrade plan. They also have resources for all the above major uses individually.

Home Solar and Other Renewables

As demonstrated in the prior chapter, clean renewables are increasingly affordable. I make special mention of solar power here since it has finally become a clean energy source that is practical for so many of us. There has been tremendous growth in adoption of this technology because it is more efficient and less expensive so it can now compare favorably to conventional energy and utility bills. In the last ten years, solar panel efficiency has improved from below 10% to at least 20%. During the same time, cost has declined at least 60% according to some sources. How much solar is best for you depends on your region, your needs, incentives and state of technology which is rapidly changing. Where I live it is normally recommended to install enough solar for most of your total home demands and remain linked to the grid. This will take care of your peak needs, allows you to use grid energy when solar is not producing at night, and when you are not producing excess energy in case there is little or no reimbursement from your utility. Home battery storage is an increasingly viable option for storing surplus production during peak hours so you can be more self-sufficient during nighttime and cloudy weather. My rooftop solar currently provides about 80-90% of my home energy needs. I may add more panels after adding battery storage which can save surplus production for other times.

While solar is a great choice especially in "sunbelt regions", other renewables are also becoming cost-effective options in most regions. Wind turbines are now in many locations where there are sustained winds. They are increasingly seen towering near interstate highways across the country. Hydro and geothermal can also serve many areas. The opportunity now for us as consumers is to create demand and help support the best technologies for our regions. The final solutions will vary according to the natural resources and infrastructure in your region.

Net Zero Home

Also termed a ZNE (zero net energy) building, the concept here is that the total amount of energy used on an annual basis by that building is met by the renewable energy (e.g. solar, wind, geothermal or some combination) produced at that property. In other words, it is energetically self-sufficient. Buildings that produce a surplus are "energy-plus", and those that consume slightly more than they produce (like mine and many others) are "near-zero energy" or "ultra-low energy." While reaching absolute ZNE can be quite costly and/or technically challenging, it can still be quite worthwhile to strive for this goal. Dramatic improvements can be made with improved HVAC, insulation and lighting, as well as the installation of renewable energy. I have been involved in large retrofit projects which have reduced energy consumption by at least 50%, and also installed solar to meet most of the reduced needs. They are so cost effective they pay for themselves in just a few years. These examples demonstrate that for both private homes and businesses, some key cost-effective measures can lead to significant improvements and long-term cost savings.

Two university-based home projects demonstrate what is already technically feasible and rapidly becoming cost-effective. The first is Harvard HouseZero (https://harvardcgbc.org/research/housezero/). The building selected for this is pre-1940s to demonstrate that the retrofits in this project can be applied to existing buildings. The overarching objective is to greatly reduce energy demand with ultra-efficient designs. Rooftop solar provides the modest energy needs for a geothermal heat pump and other equipment. A battery storage system is used for nighttime and cloudy conditions. Four major performance goals are 1) no HVAC since almost zero energy is needed for heating/cooling, 2) 100%

natural ventilation, 3) 100% natural daytime lighting, and 4) zero carbon emissions.

The outdoor climate for the Harvard HouseZero ranges from hot and humid summers to very cold winters. The second home project, the Honda Smart Home (https://www.hondasmarthome.com/), West Village in northern California has much lower seasonal fluctuations. Built new in 2014, it also has technologies which are already more broadly available to reach both zero energy and emissions goals. And it also combines rooftop solar with battery storage and a geothermal heat pump system. Beyond that, it differs in many details including materials used. It includes electric vehicle charging for a Honda FitEV (of course) which is part of a sophisticated HEMS (Home Energy Management System) that integrates with the rest of the home and the larger electrical grid. Finally, since summers are hot and dry, it features xeric landscaping and a small rain garden. The Honda Smart Home website provides updates and detailed performance data for this project.

Toward Self-Sufficiency With Clean Energy

Ideally, we can all reliably use clean energy generated on our properties or at least locally. Two major factors are pushing us in this direction. First, utilities may not be keeping up with technological improvements which can meet our needs for reliable clean energy. In California, PG&E is the largest utility. For PG&E residents, rates can be much higher than in smaller service areas of public utilities. In addition, they are being subjected to energy outages during peak winds and fire dangers. Fortunately, there are increasingly affordable solutions down to the consumer level. Beyond generating our own clean energy and using it much more efficiently (as outlined above), we can also store it for use overnight, during power outages and other emergencies. Here are some examples:

- Battery storage systems: at least 17 major brands include Equana (12.1 kWh), Panasonic (5.7-17.1 kWh) and Tesla (13.5 kWh). According to the Tesla website, their system "can run an average home for about 8 hours." Thus, limiting use to key emergency equipment could last longer.

- Plug-in cars generally have batteries ranging from 10-100 kWh. This can be an alternative to gasoline-powered generators. One example is the EV733 home lifeline generator (see website of California Sunlight) which can run devices of up to 1000W at up to 4 kWh per day. It has an optional portable solar panel as the power source.

One important housing trend is that a greater proportion of US households are now renting. The percentage has reached 37 overall, and it is much higher at 65% for those under the age of 35 (http://www.pewresearch.org). Fortunately, there are more options for renters as well as homeowners as described below.

Sustainable Communities

Beyond your home and property, there are many great examples of how your neighborhood can promote and enhance sustainable communities. The term "community" has been applied to a broad range of groups on up to various international "communities." Here we focus on local developments where design can significantly impact the amount and quality of interactions with your neighbors. One interesting discussion of community size concludes that the optimum is about 500 people or 150 homes (Corbett and Corbett 1999, p. 139). This section describes some northern California communities in that size range where I have lived and visited. The first is Village Homes described in detail in the box below.

**Village Homes.** Beginning in 1985, I had the opportunity to live in Village Homes, Davis, for many years. This is one of the original "sustainable communities" which started in the 1970s (Corbett and Corbett 2000). Many features are well ahead of their time, and they are gaining greater mainstream acceptance and appreciation. Here are some that residents and their guests enjoy:

- _Homes with passive solar designs that include large south-facing windows and glass doors, and roof overhangs that allow solar heating in winter, and shade in the summer. These and other features also provide natural lighting and ventilation. Many of these designs predate and complement the more recent technological improvements listed above._

- _Designated areas for those who want to grow food. These range from large community gardens to small individual raised bed plots (Figure 8.2A, B). Other parts of the "edible landscape" include fruit orchards (Figure 8.2C) and herbs maintained by Village Homes staff and harvested by residents._

- _Paths that allow safe walking and biking throughout the development as an alternative to cars (Figure 8.2C)._

Figure 8.2. Village Homes, California. A. Large community garden area, and B. Small raised bed plot

- *Recharge of the local groundwater and aquifer with canals and seasonal holding ponds (Figure 8.2D) instead of a stormwater system that exports water during the rainy season.*

The shared edible landscape, paths and lack of fences between properties all contribute to more positive interactions among neighbors. This is confirmed by both my anecdotal experiences over the years and more formal social science research (see Corbett and Corbett 1999 for more detailed discussions).

Figure 8.2 Village Homes, California. C. Path for walking and biking with orchard on left side, and D. Low-lying area that is also seasonal holding pond that recharges the local aquifer.

124

The developers of Village Homes have since built housing at smaller scales that add the more recent technologies available for much more efficient temperature control, insulation, lighting, solar power, etc. West Village is UC-Davis housing for students and staff that also includes many of these features for a net zero lifestyle. The above-mentioned Honda Smart Home is one example within this development. West Village is designed as the largest planned "zero net energy" community in the United States (https://westvillage.ucdavis.edu/). Over two thousand residents are able to experience this lifestyle affordably.

Cohousing

Related to this, there is rapidly growing interest in cohousing. It is very interesting to consider the factors leading to this including desires for a greater sense of community and the limits of conventional developments with separate single-family homes. McCamant and Durrett (2011) provide a very thorough summary for dozens of locations in both North America and Europe. They emphasize that while intentional communities can be based on ideologies and charismatic leaders, cohousing has no ideology and emphasizes participation by all residents. While there is a great diversity of cohousing (size, location, etc.), McCamant and Durrett list six common characteristics they all share. These are listed here in bold, followed by my comments:

- **Participatory Process.** Residents are involved from the start, beginning with the planning and design. Thus, all can contribute to final decisions. This leads to. . .

- **Complete Residential Management.** Residents manage the development with regular meetings and committees.

- **Non-Hierarchical Structure.** This allows decisions to be made by consensus fairly and equally.

- **Designs That Facilitate Community.** This includes strategic placement of homes, paths and common areas.

- **Extensive Community Facilities.** The common house for cooking and meals can include many other features including lounge/recreation, laundry, guest rooms and studios. Additional facilities can include workshops, garage/storage, greenhouses and more recreational facilities.

- **Separate Income Sources.** Residents own their homes and a share of the common areas, so the financial arrangement resembles a condominium.

Beyond these broad similarities, it is quite interesting to see how these projects can adjust to the unique local resources and social needs of their locations. All this is discussed in great detail in McCamant and Durrett (2011).

Housing – My Actions Toward Sustainability

Daily:

Short Term:

Long Term:

Chapter Nine

MOBILITY

————

While housing is generally the most expensive item for most family budgets, transportation including the commute and other mobility needs is normally second. Cars have become especially central for those living in suburban single-family dwellings. This is historically considered a key to the American Dream we all aspire to. Cars reflect our standard of living, and they represent our freedom to pursue a better life. They can be a key means to upward mobility. I certainly appreciate the many opportunities that cars, planes and other mobility have provided or enhanced in the many countries I have lived in over the years. Greater access to mobility is compatible with the theme of abundance in the other chapters. There are now many ways we can all contribute to minimizing environmental impacts and participating in more convenient mobility for all.

Two main mobility concerns are air pollution from vehicle emissions and congestion from increasing traffic that lengthens commutes and makes parking difficult. The simple solution advocated by many is to replace your car with walking, biking or taking mass transit to work. Unfortunately, this is not practical for many if not most of us. For decades most development has been car-centric, so we need new or revised urban and suburban designs to allow for greater use of these alternatives. Much of this is underway. Meanwhile, there is still much we can do as consumers. First, we can reduce and even eliminate emissions in our mobility. Second, we can demand and support the alternatives that are rapidly developing. This chapter reviews these options in that order.

We are now in the midst of enormous changes in how we can move about. Three especially important "revolutions" are electrification, increasingly automated (including driverless) vehicles, and ride sharing (Sperling 2018). All these provide us additional opportunities for more sustainable lifestyles. Fortunately for consumers, there have recently been great improvements in performance, reliability, and cost of greener vehicles. There are also many interesting and promising alternatives to traditional car ownership that are developing. This chapter focuses on electrification since it can be based on clean and renewable energy. This is foundational for solving our climate change and local air pollution with proven technologies. Automation and ride sharing can enhance the benefits of electrification while greatly reducing congestion and the need for parking. These three groups of technologies can be combined in various ways, so you can choose new mobility options that fit your needs and lifestyle.

Our Current Mobility

It is helpful to begin with putting traditional driving in context with other mobility and emerging alternatives. Table 9.1 provides a summary of our key mobility patterns.

Table 9.1. USA per capita mobility averages from various sources.

• 90% of our motorized travel is by private car. About 8% is by airplane, and less than 1% each is by bus and train.
• We walk an average of 3000-4000 steps (1.5-2 miles) per day.
• 12% of us bike regularly 4-6 miles daily.
• The average daily car commute is 29.2 miles

In the USA, 90% of our motorized travel is by private car (see Wikipedia Mode of Transport, section on worldwide comparisons). This is followed by airplane (about 8%), and then by bus and railway (both less than 1%). Globally, per capita travel by car is much lower, but it is still much higher than the per capita travel via bus, rail and air. For human-powered travel, USA averages are 3000 to 4000 steps per day (about 1.5-2 miles) for walking, and about 4-6 miles for the 12% of people who bike regularly. We can also compare the emissions for all the above. While there is much variability due to the range of vehicles and types of power used, some generalizations can be made. For motorized travel, trains (especially), full cars, buses and motorbikes have lower emission rates. The highest rates are from cars with 1-2 people, planes, trucks and ships (Wikipedia – Environmental impact of transport). Thus, it is clear that the main way we get around, in cars just by ourselves, also pollutes the most. This is the key opportunity for improvement. Fortunately, solutions are becoming available.

We can focus on our main daily transportation need: getting to and from work and errands. The overall average in the US is 29.2 miles per person for a roundtrip commute. For most of us (over 77%) this commute is 20 miles or less. Thus, the relative few that drive well over 30 miles/day drive up the overall average.

Electrification Of Our Mobility

For the vast majority of us that drive well under 30 miles per day, even the electric vehicle (EV) technologies of past models with ranges of 40-60 miles are sufficient. Now there are affordable models with ranges well over 200 miles, so most of us can now choose a model which eliminates the "range anxiety" of models with low range. Since 2010, electric vehicles (EVs), like solar for housing, have made quantum improvements in performance and reliability at lower costs. For example, there are affordable models available with ranges over 200 miles and fast charging capabilities. There are also greater opportunities for solar and EV technologies to be combined to enhance each other. The home can be the major source of clean renewable energy for your electric vehicle. In turn, with developing vehicle to grid (V2G) technologies your EV can provide battery storage capacity for peak demands, nighttime and blackouts. So, this chapter shows how to evaluate your EV needs using the common currencies of kWh and kW. Then it summarizes new opportunities including autonomous vehicles. Finally, it concludes by merging these with the whole range of clean mobility options, from walking and biking to much larger transport including buses, trains and planes.

A major concern is how long it takes to charge an EV. For most commuting needs even the slowest 120V charging from a typical outlet (4-6 miles per hour) gives you 30 miles of range in 5-7.5 hours. Thus, there is plenty of time for even this slowest "trickle" charging overnight at home, and/or while at work. There are many models available which can charge much faster even at home: up to 25 miles/hour at 240V. All this confirms that we already have proven technologies for the vast majority of our commuting needs. Your home can be the most convenient location for commuter charging.

For longer road trips, the rapidly expanding fast charging infrastructure allows electric vehicles to travel hundreds of miles per day and recharge reasonably quickly. There are two major networks: Tesla supercharging, and DC fast charging. There are many full-electric models which can charge at least 80 miles/hour with 480V DC fast charging. In a recent trip (summer of 2020) I was able to add about 150 miles of range within 40 minutes to a Tesla at a supercharging location. Every year we see more new models with greater range, and faster-charging infrastructure. This makes long distance travel, even across the country, more feasible and convenient.

One key to appreciating what EVs can do is to use the units emphasized in the last two chapters, especially kWh. Most people still think in terms of miles per gallon, which does not apply for full electric vehicles especially. MPGe (miles per gallon equivalent) can also be very confusing since it uses conversion factors which may not be accurate. So, I demonstrate here how cost effective and convenient EVs can be for the average EV driving the average commute. Most EVs can drive 3-4 miles per kWh. A "lead foot" who is always using the instant torque of the EV may get less than 3 miles, while a "hyper miler" can certainly get well over 4 miles, especially in stop and go traffic. So, we can choose an overall average of 3.5 miles/kWh. Thus, only about 8.3 kWhs are needed for a 29-mile daily commute. Many utilities have very low off-peak charging rates. For example, mine is about 7 cents per kWh (see section below for a summary of my electric vehicle after nine years of driving). Thus, for this 29-mile commute I only pay 7x8.3= 58 cents if I average 3.5 miles/kWh. My actual average is closer to 3.8 miles/kWh, so I pay only about 53 cents for the average 29-mile commute using clean renewable energy!

The above demonstrates how economical electric vehicles can be for commuting. For those concerned about what an EV adds to your electricity use and costs, Figure 9.1 provides a comparison for the EV and other major home uses Here EV energy use is well below the two major energy needs, and only about 12% of the total. This example shows about 2400 kWh for the EV per year, which at the above off-peak rate is about $168/year, or only about $14 per month! This comes quite close to my monthly average of about $12.50 per month. All this

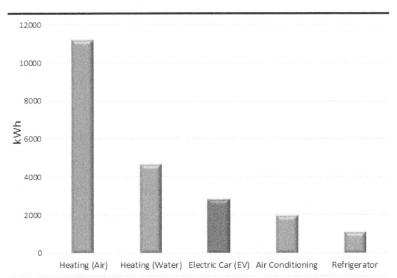

Figure 9.1. Average annual USA household energy use of electric vehicles compared with other major home needs. Data source: Office of Energy Efficiency And Renewable Energy (2017).

demonstrates that establishing your home as the main source of renewable energy for your EV can be very economical.

Here are additional economic arguments that make EVs even more compelling. First, there is much less maintenance, possibly just tire rotations for at least the initial few years. There are no oil changes for full electric vehicles, and electric motors can be much more durable with fewer parts that wear. Second, there should not be a concern about total battery price, degradation and replacement costs. There was initial concern years ago about how expensive a car battery can be to replace. Current batteries, especially those with thermal management systems, are retaining charge after many years. In my case (Figure 9.2), after nearly nine years the range of my EV can still be at least 10% over the EPA estimate, with no noticeable degradation since the vehicle was new in 2011. This is confirmed by thousands of owners of this model and others with the available high-quality batteries. Thus, the cost of battery replacement is not relevant. What is much more relevant is the long-term cost of ownership over many years. At this point, my major (and sometimes only) monthly expense is the above $12.50 for charging. This confirms

Sustainability Adventure 5

My Plug-In Electric Vehicle. *My 2011 Chevrolet Volt after 9 years of driving:*

- *91159 Total Miles (77485 full electric miles, about 85%)*
- *Over 250 MPG (see Voltstats.net)*
- *$12.50 average monthly electricity cost (SMUD)*
- *Maintenance: tire rotations every 8000 miles, and oil change every 2 years (4 so far).*
- *Daily commuter, and trips to San Diego, Los Angeles, Tahoe/Reno, Portland and the San Francisco Bay area.*
- *Still up to 35-40 miles of full electric range (no noticeable loss in battery capacity over time) and about 379 miles of range with a full gas tank and charge.*

Figure 9.2. My plug-in car charging at a solar-powered off-grid station. The solar array charges batteries in the white boxes. They in turn can charge the vehicle at any time (cloudy or sunny, day or night). Source: Heath Carney

the estimates that lifetime costs of ownership are lower for EVs compared to conventional vehicles.

Fuel Cell Compared To Battery Electric

Fuel cell vehicles should be mentioned since for many years they provided the promise of zero emissions with rapid refueling and long ranges (Sperling and Gordon 2009), and there are models available. Even in California where fuel cell vehicles are supported by many incentives, there remains a key roadblock: very few fueling stations, which can be quite expensive to build. I at one point agreed that fuel cell vehicles could be a great alternative for larger vehicles and longer distances. That was with the battery technologies of ten years ago. Now with the remarkable improvements in both batteries and charging speeds, battery electric vehicles are looking much better even in some of these categories. Fuel cell systems are being developed for large commercial vehicles that must go very long distances such as airplanes. For most of us, battery electric vehicles are the most elegant and convenient for fueling with clean renewables such as solar.

V2G (Vehicle To Grid)

This refers to the battery in the vehicle being able to provide power while parked, including power to the grid during peak demand. Morris (2019) gives a good update noting there are vehicle-to-home (for example during power outages) and other building applications. Thus, the more general acronym is V2X rather than just V2G. This is not discussed in detail here since vehicles need to have bidirectional charge capability which is still not generally available. We can look forward to the development of benefits for both EV consumers and the grids they use.

While electrification of cars can help solve regional to global emissions issues, it does not solve congestion and parking issues. To solve these additional problems, electrification can be combined with ride sharing and automation. Here are some alternatives you can look for and support as they are developing:

Autonomous

Burns and Shulgan (2018) give an excellent historical account of advances which are leading to driverless vehicles. Like many technologies including the internet, computers and jet engines, many of the advances for these vehicles were supported with U.S. military support with their applications in mind. Several DARPA (Defense Advanced Research Projects Agency) Challenge competitions between 2004 and 2007 lead to highly functional driverless vehicles. Then there were trials on actual streets such as Google Chauffeur In 2009, and the first fully driverless ride on a public road was by a blind man in a Google Firefly in 2015. Safety has of course been a major concern, and autonomous technologies have developed to the point of being much safer than humans in the major types of accidents. I certainly look forward to the elimination of human error such as drunken and distracted driving. During the past decade we have seen more key technical elements added to new vehicles every new model year. This includes sensors and cameras which detect and show other vehicles and objects, GPS-based navigation, and adaptive cruise control. The opportunity for us as consumers and drivers is to try and enjoy these new technologies as they become available. The responsibility that comes with this is to understand their limits and stay within manufacturer recommendations. For example, the first Tesla vehicles with autopilot were still not fully driverless. During this transition, we should understand what a given vehicle can and can't do while we look forward to our first fully driverless ride in the near future.

Shared

This is an area where we are seeing many more options. One of the most significant is ride sharing of private vehicles by Uber and Lyft which are challenging both conventional taxis and rental cars. Both of these companies have plans to integrate the other two revolutions of electrification and driverless vehicles. So, we can all look forward to being able to summon a driverless electric vehicle with our smartphones. Personally, I especially look forward to clean electric sharing. With a broad view of sharing, Uber is also working on electric VTOLs in urban areas. Another interesting program in my region is GIG/AAA. They have placed hundreds of full electric vehicles on the streets of Sacramento and San Francisco. After a quick registration process, you can use their smartphone app to reserve and locate the vehicle closest to you and then use it for anything from a quick one-way trip within a certain region to shopping and errands to multi-day trips. There are also many ingenious systems in developing countries that have been born of the absolute necessity for affordable mobility. For example, in Bolivia, one of the poorest countries in Latin America, I recall the popular "quinienteros." These were privately owned vehicles serving major routes, a simple pre-Uber without the apps, and often filled with passengers. With a diversity of systems and technologies, we can support mobility alternatives that are both cleaner and more affordable.

One final alternative deserves some discussion: electrification of "micromobility" including scooters, bikes and skateboards. In principle this can be a great alternative for getting from a transit center or parking lot to your final destination. My concern is safety, especially for both pedestrians and micromobility users in crowded urban areas. One solution already in place in certain areas is banning use of these vehicles in sidewalks and other pedestrian areas. This still leaves the problem of accidents of users on roads and paths, much as for motorcycles. Personally, I favor walking. Longer walks are that much more exercise we can all benefit from!

Electrification of Other Major Modes of Transport

The remarkable improvements noted above in battery capacity, efficiency and charging are also applied to larger commercial vehicles. Here are some highlights we are beginning to see and can look forward to:

- **Buses:** 100% electric buses are already being added to fleets including municipalities, schools and airports. In 2019, the vast majority of these buses were operating in China (Marshall 2019). Their use is growing rapidly in other countries including the USA. In 2018 the Mayors of the major California cities called for the conversion to electric buses, and that has been mandated statewide by 2029. Major companies already building EV buses there include BYD and Proterra.

- **Trucks And Vans:** Tesla is developing the medium duty Cybertruck pickup (250+ mile range) and the heavy-duty Semi (300- or 500-mile range). Other brands include Rivian, Bollinger, Ford and General Motors (Gorzelany 2019). Many companies are electrifying their delivery and cargo van fleets. One notable recent example is the well-publicized effort by Amazon to electrify their fleet with thousands of delivery vans. Other companies include FedEx, DHL, USPS, Ryder and UPS. This is already proving very cost effective since van batteries and charging can be customized to very predictable delivery routes. Add this to the lower cost of ownership for electric vehicles for a very compelling alternative for fleet managers. Meanwhile we can support the health benefits and green efforts of these companies.

- **Trains:** there is a long history of electrification with technologies that include overhead lines or third rails powering electric motors, and electro-diesel locomotives for non-electrified routes. Electrification is much more cost effective when more traffic within shorter distances justifies the additional infrastructure, so we can look forward to more in urban regions especially.

- **Airplanes And VTOLs:** many smaller electric airplane models are already operating in regional markets (Morris 2017). This includes both full electrics and plug-in hybrids with ranges of up to 600-700 miles. VTOL (Vertical Take-Off and Landing) vehicles are particularly well suited for large urban areas since they do not require large runways. They can begin with existing infrastructure such as heliports, which can lead to more extensive networks of "vertiports." Uber has started a substantial program at a global level (Holden and Goel 2019). Large fuel cell-powered airplanes are being developed by major manufacturers including Airbus for long-distance flights.

- *Boats:* historically, electric boats (like electric cars) were quite popular during the late 1800s and early 1900s until internal combustion engines became dominant. In recent decades, interest and use of electric boats has increased for the same reasons as for all the other land and air vehicles above. They are especially feasible and desirable for shorter trips in urban areas and inland waterways.

In summary, our mobility options and technologies are rapidly improving and changing. Electric vehicles have longer ranges, faster and more convenient charging, and lower costs. We can also look forward to the electrification of other modes including buses, trucks, vans, taxis, boats, trains and even planes. We can support all of these, and their use of local and regional clean renewable energy sources. The technology for autonomous vehicles has already arrived, and test fleets are in operation. This can be combined with ride sharing in new ways. For example, we may be able to share an autonomous commuter. We may be able to rent one for a single one-way trip (say to the airport) or a road trip. There will be many sustainability opportunities to drive more efficiently using the clean renewable energy produced in that region. Ideally congestion will be reduced by integrating these technologies with improved mass transport. We should all support and look forward to clean, safe and care-free mobility.

Mobility – My Actions Toward Sustainability

Daily:

Short Term:

Long Term:

Chapter Ten

SUSTAINABLE SEXUALITY AND

POPULATION

———————

O ur global human population is critical to the quality of sustainability we can reach. To simply survive at a very basic level and perpetuate the species, we can reach and maintain a relatively high population level. However, more resources per capita are needed for quality sustainability that includes education, the technologies discussed in the last two chapters, and living standards we all aspire to including quality food, water, housing, mobility and open spaces. The global population is nearly 7.8 billion at the writing of this chapter in 2020 (see for example the Worldometer live link: http://www.worldometers.info/world-population/ for the most current estimates when you read this). The global human carrying capacity is the population that can be sustained by global resources. There are many estimates for this carrying capacity. Most range from about 4 billion to 16 billion people. This large variation is understandable given the assumptions we must make about the resources available, and what quality of life they can support. Still, the consensus is that not more than 10 billion can be supported by global resources (see, for example, Wilson 2002). By comparison, a more recent estimate for an optimal human population is 1.5 to 2 billion (Vidal 2012 interview of Paul Ehrlich). Our current global population is already well over these estimates. The global population is now growing at about 1.05% per year. At this rate we will reach the 10 billion level at about 2057 (see Worldometer for updated estimates).

This remarkable population growth and level is ultimately fueled by our individual sexual drives and decisions multiplied by billions. Our innate biology gives us the opportunity to have large families when healthy and with sufficient resources. A sustainability perspective should help inform and improve cultural and religious norms about sexuality, birth and families so we all have opportunities for productive and meaningful lives within the global carrying capacity. The poorer developing countries have the highest birth rates (Sachs 2015), so that is where there is the greatest need to develop resources such as education and health care. That is also where there is the greatest need and potential to transition directly to clean energy sources from within those regions. The same can be said for the poorer parts of both rural and urban USA.

The key reasons for high population growth are clear: unplanned and unwanted births. And the consequences are enormous. This is a root cause of our major social problems including terrorism, gun violence and other serious crimes. All of these are concentrated in poor areas where parents and children do not have access to more positive and productive alternatives. Thus, we need to understand and better manage birth rates. The reason for high birth rates is deeply rooted in our biology. Our capacity for sex is much greater than is needed for even a large family. Some estimates are that the average person can have sex over 5000 times in their lifetime. This is considered healthy and normal, and obviously can quickly lead to pregnancy many times over. Historically, high births were balanced by high mortality at all stages from infant to childhood to adult. Now the high mortality is being reduced in even the poorest regions with at least the basic nutrition and medical care needed for basic survival. Still, a child clearly needs much more than this for a productive and happy life. This includes education, family and community support, a healthy living environment, and productive job opportunities. Cultural and religious norms in many regions are woefully outdated and inadequate to keep pace with these rapidly changing needs and opportunities.

At the individual level, sustainability can inform human sexuality and family planning. It does so by balancing and reconciling our sex drives with our need to limit and plan for those born so they have the opportunity for quality lives. So, there should be no social or religious limits to birth control techniques before, during or immediately after sex (ideally well before there is a fetus). Licenses and training should be considered for having children even more than for getting married. After all, consider the enormous social costs of unwanted and/or unplanned births. And also consider the tremendous benefits of thoughtful planning and adequate resources. I am certainly grateful for all that my parents were able to provide for my brothers, sister and me. This even included college trust funds which allowed us to get our college educations without going into debt. Having sex can have many biological and social benefits in addition to procreation. It can help with social bonding, and also provides physical and emotional benefits. So, the emphasis should be placed on limiting the births to what is wanted and can be supported by the parents. Fortunately, there is a trend toward lower birth rates and more quality childhoods as we become more educated and developed. Globally, there is a declining birth rate which ideallly will reach steady state when we are at carrying capacity. Thus, the religious and cultural norms discussed in the earlier chapters need to be updated to meet our ever-greater needs and opportunities.

The greatest progress towards sustainability is made when individuals and couples can plan, conceive and bring up children with adequate resources. The foundation for this has three pillars:

- First, base our attitudes and actions on scientific information rather than outdated myths and misinformation. This includes the biology of sexual drives and function, birth control, pregnancy and children.

- Second, with family planning have adequate resources so that newborn children can have the best possible start in life. There is increasing evidence that many of the most important biological, psychological and social developments take place in the first years of our lives, even before formal education begins.

- Third, stretch those resources to entire lifetimes. This includes supporting physical and mental well-being at every stage in life. Adopting the lifestyle improvements in the earlier chapters helps us get there. If we can all reduce waste and use renewables then there will be that much more to share with others.

With the above, we can identify improvements, especially in lower-income and otherwise disadvantaged areas, at the following stages:

- *Before sex and birth:* more educational resources for healthy intimacy, safe sex, and family planning. The benefits of non-sexual intimacy and safe sex should be emphasized. For those who do want children, licensing should be considered. It is critical for parents to understand what is involved, and the resources they will need.
- *During sex:* knowledge of the best techniques and supplies(toys) for mutual sexual satisfaction. Ideally this will have the desired outcome in both intimacy and birth control.

- *After conception:* resources that will lead to happy and productive lives. For very low-income children there needs to be a safety net of adequate nutrition, education and health services. For unwanted children it is critical to identify and minimize abuse and/or neglect at the earliest possible time so that mental damage and criminal behavior can be avoided.

Table 10.1 summarizes the key parts of sex lives for people living in the USA. For both male and female, the average age of first sex is 17. For teenage females, unwanted pregnancies are fortunately gradually declining, but the percentage out of marriage is increasing due to older age of marriages. Frequency of sex can reach over twice per week in our twenties and thirties, and then usually gradually declines with age. Masturbation can reach the same levels, but for very different reasons according to gender. For men, masturbation generally compensates for a lack of partnered sex, whereas for women it complements partnered sex. Births per couple declined to 1.73 lifetime as of 2018, which is about 18% below the level needed for the population to replace itself (Hamilton 2020). Thus, the USA joins other developed countries (mainly in Europe and Asia) with lower than replacement values.

Still, global rates are higher due to higher birth rates in developing countries. In the USA abortion rates are also declining, down to 24% per female over her lifetime. For permanent birth control, about 25% of women choose tubal ligation, while only 10% of men choose vasectomy. Since vasectomies are very quick and cost effective, more men should consider this option when the time is right.

Table 10.1. Summary of key parts of one's sex life in the USA.

Age of first sex	17 (both female and male)
Unwanted pregnancies	about 50%
Frequency of sex with partner	1-2 times per week, gradual decline with age
Frequency of masturbation	monthly to weekly by vast majority in USA and globally
Per capita births during lifetime	1.73 per couple in 2018, declining annually
Per capita abortions during lifetime	0.24 in 2017, declining annually
Percentage end procreation	Female tubal ligation: 25% Male vasectomy: 10%

Estimates of averages are from various sources including Wikipedia https://en.wikipedia.org/wiki/Adolescent_sexuality_in_the_United_States and Planned Parenthood https://www.plannedparenthood.org/about-us/facts-figures.

Sexuality – My Actions Toward Sustainability

Daily:

Short Term:

Long Term:

Chapter Eleven

CONCLUSION: CONNECTING TO OUR COMMUNITIES AND BIOREGIONS

We can conclude with a summary of how applying sustainability at the individual level as demonstrated in this book can improve our lives and those we are in contact with. One major reason I have included many positive examples and practices in each chapter is to demonstrate there is something for everyone here. Some, especially those young and starting out, may only have the time and resources for the relatively easy and inexpensive practices such as food choice and water use. I maintain there is still much you can do for both yourself and others at this level. Then you can graduate to owning the greenest options for home and transportation. Finally, time and resources allowing, you can make your goal self-sufficiency based on clean renewable energy. Some of these options can be quite expensive and/or time consuming. On the other hand, this book shows that some of the most significant improvements can be relatively simple and inexpensive. One key is to simply be aware of our major types of resource use, and then apply technological and/or behavioral improvements as we can.

The previous chapters have provided a solid conceptual and scientific foundation for continuous improvement towards sustainability which you can act on immediately. I emphasize the process rather than specific end points since we all have unique circumstances and needs. It is great to establish and reach goals such as personally converting to organic foods, clean energy and wise water use. Still, there is always room for improvement which will lead to an even higher quality of sustainability. For example, once you are self-sufficient, you can contribute more to the community, which in turn feeds back to you. Ideally, your efforts are part of something much larger and over generations. This is the key way we can integrate individual sustainability with our communities and regional self-sufficiency. In my case, I started with a special opportunity to promote electric vehicles where I live. This led to related work on clean energy sources for both home and vehicle. I have participated in local and regional events. One has led to another, and before you know it you become connected to the regional sustainability network which includes all the key elements covered in the earlier chapters. This is how your sustainability efforts can grow "organically", tuned uniquely to your region, and constantly adjusting as conditions change (Figure 11.1).

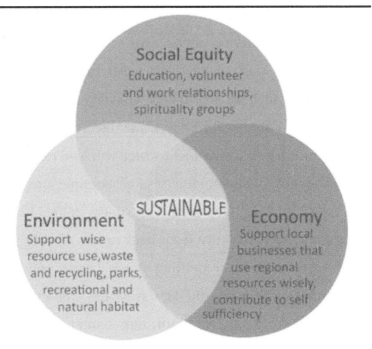

Figure 11.1. How the individual can contribute to sustainability at the community and regional levels.

Here especially we should emphasize process rather than results or end points which can quickly become outdated. We need to be flexible and opportunistic for two major reasons. First, how far we can go depends entirely on the circumstances in a given region. The best solutions are uniquely local, tuned to the natural and cultural resources, and to the economic conditions of that region. Desert, forest, mountain and coastal regions should all have distinct clean energy, food and water use solutions tailored to their resources which the individuals and communities living there can best manage. Second, we should be able to adjust to improving technologies and changing conditions. I have featured how much more practical and accessible new clean technologies including solar, wind and electric vehicles are. There is still much work needed to make all these mainstream realities.

This is how we can add to sustainability progress in the coming years: a grassroots "bottom up" approach featuring local and regional champions who are living by example and working for the best solutions for their regions. This can merge with existing "top-down" regional, national and global programs initiated by the leaders and managers at these levels. Ideally, this will have two major outcomes:

- First, unique solutions for each region grow organically from the experience and commitment of champions. This will reflect the unique integration of regional natural resources, cultural factors and demographics.

- Second, there is a process in place for continuous improvement, rather than a static endpoint. This is consistent with a dynamic sustainability which can adjust to constantly changing resources, technologies and demographics.

When circumstances can seem overwhelming at the higher regional to global levels, we can go back to the individual level where sustainability efforts are ALWAYS possible as long as we put in the effort, and then proceed to the local and regional levels from there.

To summarize and visualize all your sustainability goals, you can now do a second assessment to quantify and visualize your goals (Figure 11.2). Rate how your goals will improve each category in the self-assessment of Table 1.1. You may want to break this down into short term vs. long term as shown in Figure 11.2. This allows for both immediate actions and more long-term projects.

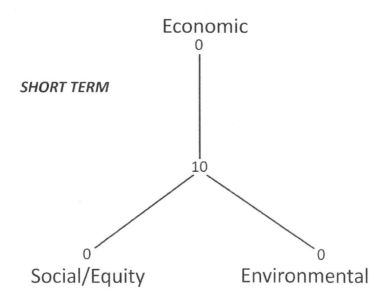

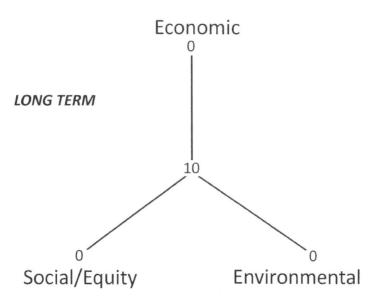

Figure 11.2. Graph of your sustainability goals. This is divided into the relatively easy daily and short term vs. more time consuming and long term as you have listed for each chapter.

You can then monitor and periodically update these assessments. For example, you can make this part of your New Year's resolutions.

Connecting To Your Community

Much has been written about community in relation to sustainability since they are mutually reinforcing. Amongst the areas covered in this book, you can choose how to contribute more to your community. This can greatly enhance progress on Environment and Economy, and is central to improving Equity. Wendell Berry (1995) provides seventeen guiding principles for strengthening communities with a sustainability foundation. He emphasizes the value of agrarian communities with local food-based economies. Thus, he picks up where I leave off with this book. My book sets the foundation for you at the individual level. You can then continue on to the larger community level with Berry (1995), Carroll (2004) and many others.

Connecting To Your Bioregion and Ecoregion

Bioregions are defined by biological rather than political criteria and boundaries. This can allow for a better integration of natural resources with economic and equity issues within a given bioregion. Ecoregions are within bioregions and they are defined by distinctive geography and assemblages of natural plants, animals and other species. Robert Thayer (2003) advocates for bioregions using the Sacramento Valley bioregion and Putah-Cache watershed he has lived in for many decades as a key example. He makes the case that this is the most logical scale for a sustainable community to take root and flourish. He has lived in Village Homes and wrote the foreword on this development by Corbett and Corbett (2000). So, his book is one approach for you to link what we have covered with your larger region.

Vital Role Of Sustainability In Education

Worldwatch (2017) provides a very comprehensive update on how education for sustainability and resilience can be brought together for "EarthEd" to meet our modern educational needs. Sixty-three educational experts contribute to this excellent summary. Their broad coverage of this vital topic includes children to adults, academic and vocational, and a diverse range of subjects relevant to sustainability. Erik Assadourian, the Director for the EarthEd Project, summarizes current progress: "Although many governments have made some effort to integrate education for sustainable development (ESD) into their national curricula, few have deeply integrated sustainability to the extent needed to tackle the challenges ahead." He then discusses United Nations goals, especially "Goal 4...which aims to... increase their attention to sustainability and resilience education."

Within this broader educational context, this book is written for adult and introductory undergraduate (general education) readers (as outlined in the Foreword). The main goal of a liberal arts education is to provide a basic comprehension of three key areas: natural sciences, social sciences and humanities (literature and arts). This allows us to more fully understand, participate and contribute to society. In this book I have made the case for how vital sustainability has become for us to understand and help solve our most urgent issues. The best solutions involve bringing together all the above three major pillars of a liberal arts education in the most meaningful and relevant ways. Thus, sustainability should be on the top of the list for improving undergraduate curricula, beginning with an introductory general education course for all students. Al Gore (1992) cites how important just one science course taught by Roger Revelle was for him as an undergraduate majoring in government. This was clearly critical for his efforts to raise awareness about climate change and promote effective national and global programs.

There are many more specialized courses and career paths which are already growing rapidly for both undergraduate and graduate programs (Worldwatch 2017). Matson, Clark and Andersson (2016) provide additional thoughtful discussions of how sustainability can be integrated into higher education. They describe powerful tools such as systems analysis for larger complex systems. They also outline how basic and applied research can be developed and balanced with a 4-square assessment.

Beyond that, this subject remains vital throughout our lives. We can all apply at least some of the practices in these chapters to immediately improve our lifestyles, and to promote greater awareness in our communities. All this makes it much easier to gain broad support for national and global sustainable development goals outlined by the United Nations (United Nations 2020).

Beyond Partisan Politics

Sustainability is a subject that is too important to be subjected to partisan politics. Indeed, it can be a key solution to our political polarization and divide. Many of the ideas and technologies presented here are considered by some to be aligned more with liberal Democratic perspectives and efforts. In reality, sustainability solutions benefit all of us and are quite compatible with recent conservative and Republican thinking. This is demonstrated by a comparison of the major points of several recent prominent conservative books with this one.

The first is by David Brooks, a well-known conservative commentator. In The Second Mountain (2019) he outlines how we can all lead more meaningful lives. For this, he states we need to climb two mountains during our lives. The first corresponds to the conventional American Dream described in my third chapter. The summit for that is professional and material success and independence. The second mountain requires the development of four commitments: vocation, marriage, philosophy/faith and community. In building these commitments, our lives become less self-centered, more meaningful and deeply joyful.

In my case, sustainability has provided the roadmap for climbing the second mountain with both a general framework (the three Es) and specific approaches for building commitments. I reached the first mountain with material and professional success during my thirties and forties. As predicted by Brooks, I then looked for more meaning and a greater contribution. Sustainability is a key way to scale the second mountain and contribute for positive impacts at higher levels. In summary, I find pursuing sustainability totally compatible with Brook's quest for climbing the Second Mountain.

The second book is It's Up To Us (2019) by John Kasich, Republican Governor of Ohio from 2011 to 2019 and before that Ohio State Senator and Representative. The subtitle is "ten little ways we can bring about big change." These ten principles are his foundation for a grassroots approach to larger national issues: ". . .we ought to be looking to our own houses, our own communities, and spending some time thinking about what we can do, together with our friends and family, to set the right tone for this nation, and to set us on the right path." All ten principles, and the emphasis on personal power, are quite compatible with the sustainability approaches outlined in earlier chapters. Here are three principles which are especially relevant:

- Be The Change Where You Live. The food, water, home and mobility chapters especially point to how you can focus on your home and neighborhood.
- Get Out Of Your Silo. Sustainability at its best is holistic, constantly drawing from a diverse range of

experiences and perspectives, and improved by new information and ideas.

- Spend Time Examining Your Eternal Destiny. This is consistent with the long-term multigenerational perspective of sustainability.

The third book The Vanishing American Adult (2017) is by Ben Sasse, Republican U.S. Senator for Nebraska. It focuses on the critical need to improve how young people in America are growing up to become fully functional members of our society. Sasse details five major solutions: overcome peer pressure, work hard, resist consumption, travel to experience the difference between need and want, and become truly literate. He discusses all this at the individual, family and community levels, and he devotes an entire chapter to why he has avoided going to the level of policy at the state and national levels. This is consistent with my approach to sustainability with a foundation at the personal level.

In summary, all of these conservative perspectives and priorities can be enhanced by what I have outlined to improve all of our lives. Sustainability takes you from self to selfless for your ascent of the Second Mountain. The chapters in this book detail dozens (not just ten) little ways that can contribute to big change at the national and global levels. Finally, sustainability can take a more central and vital role in education. This can give our youth the energy and tools they need for a better future.

I can add to this a very positive real-world business experience I was able to contribute to. During the past decade I worked with a large car dealership group that was beginning to sell electric vehicles and also needed facilities improvements and energy retrofits. The owners are ardent Republicans. Renovation efforts at their two largest locations with hundreds of employees resulted in improved energy efficiency of about 50%. This included LED lighting, better insulation, new HVAC, and both rooftop and parking canopy solar. At one location the new solar energy was able to meet about 80% of the total energy needs. The owner was very happy with this, and the CFO (Chief Financial Officer) was also quite happy since they recovered costs of the retrofits within a few years and have since been saving substantially on annual operating costs. All this also helped increase electric vehicle sales, so this is a great example of how green projects can benefit all of us, whatever our political affiliation.

On the liberal Democratic side, there are also many efforts to go beyond conventional politics for what unifies us. This is what Obama begins with in The Audacity of

Hope (2006). His chapter on Values could have been written by any of the above three Republicans. He recognizes the common ground in shared values including individual freedom, family and community. Many of his ideas are supported and put in practice by the sustainability approaches outlined here. Gore (2007, 2017) focuses specifically on climate change, and the sustainability practices in my chapters provide the broad framework which include the most effective climate change solutions. Finally, Newsom (2013) discusses ways we can make government more modern and effective. A sustainability perspective can certainly inform and strengthen such efforts. I have focused on the local and regional levels, and you can pick up at the state, national, and international levels with these additional authors. Ideally, modern information and technology will be combined with old-fashioned and timeless thoughtfulness and empathy. All the above authors call for listening to diverse viewpoints to bridge the Democrat-Republican divide, and then interact with respect. At the gym I try to keep in touch with the whole range of viewpoints by getting in front of the CNN and Fox News broadcasts right next to each other. It can be interesting to see how differently they can report on the same events in real time!

Sustainability, Resilience, Recent Events and the New Normal

Recent events demonstrate how sustainability and resilience are becoming increasingly important for understanding, adjusting to, and ultimately thriving in rapidly changing and new conditions. Resilience can be defined as the ability to resist or adapt to stresses such as natural and financial disasters. There is certainly a need to improve our resilience capabilities at individual to regional levels to contend with emergencies and disasters such as drought, fires, pandemics, etc. Resilience is a great complement to sustainability. Sustainability includes a broad range of positive approaches with long-term benefits. Resilience improves our ability to absorb and/or recover from minor setbacks to major catastrophes. Thus, it can preserve the gains reached through long-term sustainability efforts. The following three examples demonstrate the relevance and utility of sustainability and resilience to our most pressing issues.

The first is the novel coronavirus, or Covid19. Its rapid transmission between continents including Asia, Europe and North America underscores how our increasing global connectivity makes us much more vulnerable to pandemics. This confirms the longstanding predictions of scientific experts. A holistic and multidisciplinary approach is needed to first understand and then solve this and other pandemics. Natural science techniques can identify the origin and spread of the coronavirus. Then social science methods can contain and finally eliminate the virus. Globally, this is a complex issue quite amenable to a systems approach that integrates environmental health and economic elements for the best solutions. Equity needs to be integrated as well due to the disproportionate impacts on people of color and disadvantaged communities. We can all do our parts to contribute at the home and community levels.

The second is the death of George Floyd and related racial equality events. These underscore the importance of the third pillar of sustainability, equity. We are now more aware of such incidents, and responses can spread much more rapidly with social media connectivity. This is a very longstanding issue with many causes and solutions. One immediate priority is to emphasize awareness and positive solutions while condemning violence and looting. Historical inequalities in employment, other opportunities and policing must be addressed at all levels from local to global. Meanwhile, we can all do our part to promote equality and diversity both socially and economically.

The third is California "wildfires." They have been increasing in size and intensity in the recent decades (List of California wildfires). The four largest are since 2017 (two in 2020). Of the top twenty since 1932, half are after 2010. The reasons commonly given for these fires include the recent drought and previous fire suppression which allowed dead and dry fuel to accumulate. To these we should add increasing human population and impacts in forested areas. For example, the biggest and deadliest, the Mendocino and Camp fires, were started by human activities (ranching and faulty utility lines). Thus, they were not "wildfires" as much as fires caused by increasing human activities. And while historically fires were a regular feature of many forested regions, they are now noticed and cause more damage because people are settling in these regions.

On the surface these three examples may not appear to have any relationship to one another. However, look more deeply and we find that they have one very important common denominator. Their impacts have all been magnified by the much greater number, density and connectivity of humans in our modern world. Coronavirus has been able to spread across continents with modern air travel, and it's had the greatest impact in larger dense cities such as New York City and Los

Angeles. Social media spread news about George Floyd quickly to all parts of the world, and then enabled widespread protests and demonstrations. Wildfires have been a natural part of California landscapes, but their damage has become more extensive as humans settle and alter rural forested areas without the effective precautions we are quickly learning about from experience. Sustainability and resilience perspectives and practices are critical for addressing all these issues holistically. At larger scales sophisticated systems approaches can address complex issues for more sustainable development. We can all complement these efforts with effective action at the scale of our homes and communities. This can be as simple as wearing masks and social distancing for coronavirus. To promote equity, we can all be more positive and engaged neighbors in our increasingly diverse communities. To protect against wildfires, floods, drought, hurricanes and tornadoes, we can all pay more attention to where and how we build homes, and then take the precautions needed to keep them safer.

In conclusion, sustainability as presented here improves your health and lifestyle. This can then be the foundation for contributing at larger scales ranging from community to global. In these times of coronavirus, demonstrations for greater equality, record heat, fires and other "natural" disasters there is nothing more vital and urgent than contributing to sustainability goals with the deeply committed personal approach outlined here. Walking the sustainability talk is a tremendous opportunity for all of us as well as a responsibility to others. Using a process of continuous improvement towards sustainability, we can find better ways to integrate the three Es (Economy, Equity and Environment) with new approaches and technologies. So grow, enjoy, and prosper with all your sustainability adventures!

Community and Region – My Actions Toward Sustainability

Daily:

Short Term:

Long Term:

Bibliography

Adams, James T. 1931. *The Epic Of America*. Little, Brown & Co.

Anger, Judith, et al. 2015. Living On An Urban Homestead: An Interview With Jules Dervaes. *Mother Earth News* October.

Berry, Wendell. 1995. *Another Turn Of The Crank*. Berkeley: Counterpoint.

Blumberg, Antonia. 2014. Religious, Interfaith Organizations Put The Faith Back In Green Activism. *Huffpost* – Religion April 22.

Bowman, S.A., J. C. Clemens, J.E. Friday, N. Schroeder, M. Shimizu, R.P. LaComb, and A.J. Moshfegh. 2018. *Food Patterns Equivalents Intakes by Americans: What We Eat in America*, NHANES 2003-2004 and 2015- 2016. *Food Surveys Research Group*. Dietary Data Brief No. 20, November.

Brinkman, Robert. 2016. *Introduction to Sustainability*. Hoboken: Wiley-Blackwell.

Brooks, David. 2019. *The Second Mountain: The Quest for a Moral Life*. New York: Random House.

Brush, Stephen B., Heath J. Carney and Zosimo Huaman. 1981. Dynamics of Andean Potato Agriculture. *Economic Botany* 35(1): 70-88.

Burns, Lawrence D., and Christopher Shulgan. 2018. *Autonomy. The Quest To Build The Driverless Car-And How It Will Reshape Our World*. New York: HarperCollins.

Carney, Heath J. 1980. *Diversity, Distribution and Peasant Selection of Indigenous Potato Varieties in The Mantaro Valley: A Biocultural Evolutionary Process*. Lima, Peru: International Potato Center Social Science Department Working Paper Series 1980-3.

Carney, Heath J., Michael W. Binford, Alan L. Kolata, Ruben R. Marin and Charles R. Goldman. 1993. Nutrient and Sediment Retention in Andean Raised-Field Agriculture. *Nature* 364: 131-133.

Carney, Heath J., Robin Kozloff and Edith Cook. 1994. Raised–Field Farming. Increased Yields and Environmental Benefits. *Small Farmer's Journal* 18(2): 25-26.

Carroll, John E. 2004. *Sustainability and Spirituality.* Albany: SUNY Press.

Center for Sustainable Systems, University of Michigan. 2020. *Carbon Footprint Factsheet.* Pub. No. CSS09-05.

Corbett, Judy, and Michael Corbett. 2000. *Designing Sustainable Communities. Learning from Village Homes.* Washington D.C: Island Press.

Dhiman, Satinder, and Joan Marques. 2016. *Spirituality and Sustainability.* Switzerland: Springer International Publishing.

Dudley, Dominic. 2019. Renewable Energy Costs Take Another Tumble, Making Fossil Fuels Look More Expensive Than Ever. *Forbes* May 29.

Edwards, Andres R. 2005. *The Sustainability Revolution. Portrait of A Paradigm Shift.* Gabriola Island, Canada: New Society Publishers.

Edwards, Andres R. 2015. *The Heart of Sustainability. Restoring Ecological Balance From The Inside Out.* Gabriola Island, Canada: New Society Publishers.

Engelman, Robert. 2013. *Beyond Sustainababble. In State Of The World 2013. Is Sustainability Still Possible?* Washington, DC: Island Press.

Environmental Working Group. 2019. *EWG's Tap Water Database – 2019 Update Webpage.*

Ewald, Ellen Buchman. 1973. *Recipes For A Small Planet.* New York: Ballantine Books.

Fletcher, Kate. 2007. Slow Fashion. *The Ecologist* June 1.

Foer, Jonathan Safran. 2019. *We Are The Weather: Saving The Planet Begins At Breakfast.* New York: Farrar, Straus and Giroux.

Fuhrman, Joel. 2011. *Eat To Live.* New York: Little, Brown and Company.

Gore, Al. 1992. *Earth In The Balance. Ecology And The Human Spirit.* Boston: Houghton Mifflin Company.

Gore, Al. 2007. *An Inconvenient Truth. The Crisis Of Global Warming.* New York: Viking Rodale.

Gore, Al. 2017. *An Inconvenient Sequel: Truth To Power.* New York: Rodale, Melcher Media.

Gorzelany, Jim. 2019. Ready Or Not, Here Come Electric Pickup Trucks. *Forbes* July 2.

Hamilton, Brady E. 2020. *QuickStats: Expected Number of Births over a Woman's Lifetime — National Vital Statistics System,* United States, 1940–2018. MMWR Morb Mortal Wkly Rep 2020;69:20. DOI: http://dx.doi.org/10.15585

Hawken, Paul (ed). 2017. *Drawdown: The Most Comprehensive Plan Ever Proposed To Reverse Global Warming.* New York: Penguin Books.

Holden, J.; Goel, N. 2019. *Uber Elevate.* Available online: https://www.uber.com/elevate.pdf

Honore, Carl. 2004. *In Praise Of Slow.* Toronto: Vintage Canada.

Hyman, Mark. 2018. *Food. What The Heck Shall I Eat?* New York: Little, Brown and Company.

IUCN/UNEP/WWF. 1991. *Caring for the Earth. A Strategy For Sustainable Living.* Gland, Switzerland.

Kasich, John. 2019. *It's Up To Us: Ten Little Way We Can Bring About Big Change.* Toronto: Hanover Square Press.

Lappe, Francis Moore. 1971. *Recipes For A Small Planet.* New York: Ballantine Books.

Lazard. 2019. *Lazard's Levelized Cost Of Energy Analysis* – Version 13.0. Online PDF.

Little, Amanda. 2019 *The Fate Of Food.* New York: Harmony Books.

Maher, Bill. 2008. *Religulous (film).* Thousand Words, Lions Gate.

Marshall, Aarian. 2019. Why Electric Buses Haven't Taken Over The World-Yet. *Wired* June 7.

Matson, Pamela, William C. Clark and Krister Anderson. 2016. *Pursuing Sustainability. A Guide To The Science And Practice.* Princeton: Princeton University Press.

McCamant, Kathryn, and Charles Durrett. 2011. *Creating Cohousing: Building Sustainable Communities.* Gabriola Island: New Society Publishers.

Mez, Jesse, et al. 2017. Clinicopathological Evaluation of Chronic Traumatic Encephalopathy in Players of American Football. *JAMA* 318(4): 360–370.

Morris, Charles. 2017. Flying Electric. Both Startups And Industry Giants Are Pushing Ahead With Electric Airplanes. *Charged* 32: 46-59.

Morris, Charles. 2019. V2G Value Propositions. *Charged* 45: 82-86.

Mulligan, Martin. 2015. *An Introduction To Sustainability.* Oxon: Routledge.

Institute of Medicine. 2005. *Dietary Reference Intakes for Water, Potassium, Sodium, Chloride, and Sulfate.* Washington, DC: The National Academies Press. https://doi.org/10.17226/10925.

Newsom, Gavin. 2013. *Citizenville. How To Take The Town Square Digital And Reinvent Government.* New York: Penguin Books.

Nielsen. 2018. *Unpacking The Sustainability Landscape.* Insight Report November 9.

NPR. 2014. U.S. Lets 141 Trillion Calories Of Food Go To Waste Each Year. *Food For Thought.* February 27.

Obama, Barack. 2006. *The Audacity of Hope: Thoughts on Reclaiming The American Dream*. New York: Three Rivers Press.

Office Of Energy Efficiency And Renewable Energy. 2017. *Electric Vehicle Charging Consumes Less Energy than Water Heating in a Typical Household*. Fact #994, Vehicle Technologies Office. Department Of Energy. September 11.

Perlmutter, David, and Austin Perlmutter. 2020. *Brain Wash*. New York: Little, Brown Spark.

Pew Research Center. 2017. *More Americans Now Say They're Spiritual But Not Religious*. Factank September 6.

Portney, Kent E 2015. *Sustainability*. Cambridge: MIT Press.

Postel, Sandra. 2013. Sustaining freshwater And Its Dependents. *In State Of The World 2013. Is Sustainability Still Possible?* Washington, DC: Island Press.

Sachs, Jeffrey D. 2015. *The Age Of Sustainable Development*. New York: Columbia University Press.

Sakakeeny, Kria. 2019. World Water Day: How Far Would You Walk For Water? *Oxfam* March 21.

Sasse, Ben. 2017. *The Vanishing American Adult*. New York: St. Martin's Press.

Schultz, Thom, and Joani Schultz. 2013. *Why Nobody Wants To Go To Church Anymore*. Loveland: Group Publishing, Inc.

Sperling, Daniel, and Deborah Gordon. 2009. *Two Billion Cars: Driving Toward Sustainability*. New York: Oxford University Press.

Sperling, Daniel (ed). 2018. *Three Revolutions. Steering Automated, Shared, And Electric Vehicles To A Better Future*. Washington, DC: Island Press.

Starr, Kevin. 2005. *California: A History*. New York: Modern Library.

Sternheimer, Karen. 2015. *Celebrity Culture And The American Dream*. New York: Routledge.

Thayer, Robert L. 2003. *LifePlace: Bioregional Thought And Practice.* Berkeley: University of California Press.

Theis, Tom, and Jonathan Tomkin. 2015. *Sustainability: A Comprehensive Foundation.* Houston: Rice University OpenStax CNX.

Theriot, Edward, Heath J. Carney and Peter J. Richerson. 1985. Morphology, Ecology and Systematics of *Cyclotella andina* sp. nov. (Bacillariophyceae) From Lake Titicaca, Peru-Bolivia. *Phycologia* 24: 381-387.

United Nations Conference on Environment and Development. 1992. *Agenda 21, Rio Declaration, Forest Principles.* New York: United Nations.

United Nations Development Program. 2019. *The Heat Is On. Taking Stock Of Climate Ambition.* UNDP Global Outlook. New York: United Nations.

United Nations Environmental Program. 2019. *Healthy Planet, Healthy People.* UNEP Global Environmental Outlook 6. Cambridge: Cambridge University Press.

United Nations. 2020. *The Sustainable Development Goals Report 2020.* New York: United Nations.

U.S. Bureau of Economic Analysis. 2020. *Personal Consumption Expenditures [PCE],* retrieved from FRED, Federal Reserve Bank of St. Louis; https://fred.stlouisfed.org, September 28.

U.S. Department of Health and Human Services and U.S. Department of Agriculture. *2015–2020 Dietary Guidelines for Americans. 8th Edition. December 2015.* Available at https://health.gov

Vidal, John. 2012. Cut World Population And Redistribute Resources, Expert Urges. *The Guardian* April 26.

Wilson, Edward O. 2002. *The Future Of Life.* New York: Alfred A. Knopf.

World Bank. 2020. *"Households And NPISHs Final Consumption Expenditure (% of GPD)."* World Development Indicators, The World Bank Group. Accessed 9/27/2020.

World Commission on Environment and Development. 1987. *Our Common Future*. Oxford: Oxford University Press.

Worldwatch Institute. 2017. *EarthEd: Rethinking Education On A Changing Planet*. Washington, DC: Island Press.

In addition to the above references, the eBook version of this book has direct internet links to many of these and other resources highlighted in blue throughout the text.

About The Author

H eath Carney has over 40 years of sustainability experience that contribute to this book. This includes dozens of projects and programs, and thousands of students and consumers. With this diverse  background he combines a deep real world understanding of the consumer and the need to communicate clearly with academic rigor based on solid facts and a scientific process. His **sustainability projects** began in the 1970s. The first formally recognized as such following the 1987 Brundtland Commission was with the Graduate School of Design at Harvard University starting in the late 1980s. This grew into projects and programs with international organizations including United Nations (UNESCO, UNEP, UNDP) and World Bank, and with the United States government including Department of State, AID, USDA and NSF. He also worked in the **private sector** since the late 1990s, mainly in the areas of automotive sales, business development and training. Since 2010, he focused on electric vehicles. This lead to the 2016 California Governor's Environmental and Economic Leadership Award (GEELA) for promoting the sale and adoption of zero emission vehicles. He has published about 50 peer-reviewed articles and book chapters. His teaching has included classes (undergraduate and graduate) for up to 400 students, and workplace training for groups of up to 30-40. Invited public presentations have ranged from local to national and international. His educational background includes BS at College of William and Mary, MS at University of Michigan and PhD at University of California. He lives in the Sacramento watershed bioregion, California.

The author can be reached at greencar@surewest.net for speaking engagements, teaching/training, and other activities and projects.

Please review this book, especially on Amazon. We hope you have found the value to earn five stars, and any review is extremely important. This book is an ongoing project which will be revised, updated as needed, and improved. Thus, your reviews and comments will help future readers. You can also submit them to the above email address.

Made in the USA
Las Vegas, NV
24 December 2024

15305673R10108